TABLE OF CONTENTS

HOW TO USE THIS JOURNAL & WORKBOOK

For the best experience utilizing this journal, it is recommended to read the companion book, Don't Believe Everything You Think first (available at www.josephnguyen.org or anywhere you normally buy books online). You can still use this journal without reading it since each section contains a short description to provide the context needed to complete the exercises.

To get the most out of this journal and workbook, you'll want to first read all of the guides before beginning to fill them out. That way you know what each of them can help you with and choose to complete the one that would be most helpful for you at the time.

The 'Daily Journals' has 60 days worth of daily journals for you to fill out to help you remain grounded and aligned with the path you're meant to be on.

The next most common guides you'll be using will be the 'Non-thinking Decision-Making Process' and the 'Fear Neutralization Process', which each have 25 full blank templates.

The 'Non-thinking Decision-Making Process' can be used whenever you are making difficult decisions and do not know what to choose that would be most aligned to you.

The 'Fear Neutralization Process' can be used whenever you are experiencing any fear, anxiety, or negative emotions.

The guide you will use most often that will help you most with letting go of negative emotions in real-time will be the 'How To Let Go Of Negative Thinking Guide'. This guide is all you need in order to let go of any stress, overthinking, guilt, shame, fear, anxiety and anything that may cause psychological or emotional suffering.

It is a surprisingly simple process, but life-altering for anyone who can remember to use it whenever they experience suffering. I highly recommend you keep this one front and center so you can remember it as often as possible. Create a way for you to be able to access this specific guide while you are on the go for it to be most impactful for you. If you would like a PDF printable version of this guide, you may visit www.josephnguyen.org/negativethinkingguide.

A GUIDE TO END SUFFERING

THE ROOT CAUSE OF ALL SUFFERING

"I think and think and think, I've thought myself out of happiness one million times, but never once into it."
— Jonathan Safran Foer

Our feelings do not come from external events, but from our own internal thinking about the events. It is not the events that happen in our lives, but our interpretation of them, which causes our own suffering.

Reality is that the event happened, with no story, meaning, or interpretation of it. Any meaning or thinking we give the event is on us and that is how our perception of reality is created. It is through the interpretation of reality, which comes from narrating or thinking about what happened, that we create our own suffering. It is not what we are thinking, but that we are thinking, which is the root cause of our suffering.

Thoughts and thinking are two completely different phenomena. For us to experience the physical world, we have thoughts. Thoughts are not the root cause of suffering. They are inherently neutral and are merely a form of information. On the other hand, thinking is the act of thinking about our thoughts. It is not necessary to think about our thoughts. When we think about our thoughts, we cast our own limiting beliefs, judgments, and conditioning onto the thought, which creates our suffering.

You do not have to believe in this for it to be true. Test it for yourself to see what you experience.

When you are very stressed and anxious, how much thinking is going on in your mind? Now what emotion do you experience when you're not thinking?

The way to end our own suffering is not to try to stop thoughts, but for us to become aware that if we're suffering it is because we are thinking and to let go of the thinking. We can't control what thoughts pop into our minds, but we can control if we think about them or not.

All that is needed for you to end your own suffering is to become aware when you are thinking and that it is the root cause of your own suffering. Then set the intention to consciously let go of the thinking because you realize it is not helpful.

Without thinking, we are naturally in a state of peace. It is only when we think that we get ejected out from this innate state we all have. Equipped with this understanding, you now have the key to living an abundant life full of peace, love, and joy in the present moment.

HOW TO LET GO OF NEGATIVE THINKING

Here is a simple framework you can follow for when you are going through any sort of emotional suffering and want to let go of your thinking which is causing it. Give yourself the space and time to be able to gracefully go through the process. It is recommended to set aside 20-30 minutes in a quiet location free from distractions. An open and willing heart and mind are all you need to begin letting go of suffering.

Step 1: Remember that thinking is the root of all suffering

- Take a deep breaths to center and ground yourself in the present moment.
- Remember that if you're suffering, you're thinking.
- Remember the difference between thinking and thoughts.
  - Thinking is the act of thinking about thoughts. Thoughts are energetic blocks of information that pop into the mind and are inherently neutral. When we think, we cast our limiting beliefs, judgements, and conditions onto the thought, which causes fear, doubt, and anxiety. Thoughts are inevitable, thinking about them is unnecessary.
- Don't try to find the root cause of your suffering. Thinking is the root cause.

Step 2: Create a space for persisting negative thinking

- Allow the thinking to be there and acknowledge it for what it is. Don't fight it.
- Understand that you are not what you think or feelings themselves, but the sacred space that holds them.
- Don't be afraid to be alone with your thinking and have the courage to allow it to be in your consciousness. Welcome it in and see that the thinking just wants to be acknowledged.
- Ask yourself:
  - Does this thinking serve me? Do I want to keep suffering?
  - What is it costing me to continue to think and hold on to my thinking?
- Know that you are safe when you let go of your thinking and trust that your intuition will take over and take care of you like it always has when you allow it to.
- Once you allow them to exist in your consciousness and don't resist the feelings, you can then look beyond the feelings to see the truth behind it all.
- Every feeling contains a seed of truth in it which will help you deepen your awareness and allow you to experience life more fully.

Step 3: Trust and let go

Once you acknowledge that you are thinking, that it is the root cause of suffering and that you are safe when you let go of it, consciously intend and decide to let it go. Naturally positive emotions will arise, like peace, love, and joy. Allow yourself to enjoy these emotions in its fullness as they come up.

POTENTIAL OBSTACLES & SOLUTIONS

As you are working on letting go of your thinking, you may run into some potential obstacles that your logical mind tries to convince you of so that you keep thinking. Here are the most common tactics and tricks your mind will use to try to keep you in a state of anxiety and fear as well as their solutions.

Not wanting to let go of thinking because you think that it is what got you to where you are

While this half true, you must realize that what got you here, won't get you there. If you want to break the vicious cycle of suffering and the same self-destructive patterns repeating in your life, you'll have to do something different.

Insanity is doing the same thing over and over again, but expecting a different result. The real question is, do you want to be happy or not? If you understand that thinking is the root cause of all of your suffering and do not want to be unhappy any longer, then you will be able to make the leap of faith into non-thinking.

Lack of faith

In order for there to even be a possibility that your life could be a life filled with joy, peace, and love every single day, you must first believe that it is possible. You must believe that you are part of something much bigger that is the life force that has been taking care of you this whole time (Universe/God/intuition). There are an infinite number of variables, events, and circumstances that we can't possibly consider all of them through our thinking, yet we are here.

Somehow we have been guided and taken care of to lead us exactly to where we are today and most of it is not our own doing if we are being honest with ourselves. This is the presence of something much greater than we are that has been guiding us our whole lives. Having faith in something much bigger than we are without being able to fully comprehend it with our finite minds is the only way we can surrender our manual efforts of thinking and experience total peace in our lives versus worrying about everything.

Fear

Fear is a completely normal emotion when it comes to trusting in the Universe, which is also the unknown. Fear is an indication that something is very important to us, so this is a great sign. Everything we could ever want is on the other side of fear and deep down you know this is the truth.

The test we must pass in order to obtain all we desire is fear itself. The way out is through and going deep within yourself to see and know that you will be okay no matter what. That this fear cannot and will not kill you, but if you do not confront it, it will take the life of all your dreams instead. Thinking is the root cause of fear. If you don't think, there is no fear.

HOW TO KNOW IF YOU'RE IN A STATE OF NON-THINKING

When you're not thinking, you experience complete peace, love, joy, passion, excitement, inspiration, bliss, and any positive emotion your consciousness can be aware of.

You may be having thoughts, but you are unattached to them and are allowing them to just flow through you without any friction or pain that comes from thinking. There is no presence of psychological or emotional suffering.

You're not thinking about the past or future. They simply do not matter or exist to you because you're fully in the present moment. You feel like you're in flow, which comes from a state of non-thinking. You lose sense of time, space, and even your sense of self. You feel "one" with what you are doing and with life as a whole. This is how you know you are not thinking.

"Non-thinking is a state of pure presence, where one is unattached to the thoughts and thinking going on in the mind."

HOW DO YOU KNOW WHAT TO DO WITHOUT THINKING?

Although there are no right or wrong decisions we can make, just like how there are no wrong keys on a piano, there are decisions or "keys" that are more pleasant than others depending on the context. Knowing that there is no right or wrong relieves us from quite a bit a pressure to "choose the right one".

When we make decisions, we want to rely on non-thinking. When we try to think, analyze, create pros and cons lists, and ask everyone (including our pets) for advice, it causes anxiety and frustration until we make the decision. Most of the time, we already know deep down what to do in any specific situation. This is often referred to as your gut feeling, intuition, or inner wisdom. What we do is try to confirm our intuition with the external world and this is where most of the negative emotions begin to surface, wreaking havoc on our mental state because of everyone's opinions.

Only you can know what you want to do. No one else can tell you this. There will be mentors and coaches that can guide you to help you along the way, but the best ones will tell you to listen to your intuition and look within yourself for the answer (the truth is only ever within you). This is why many of us experience the phenomenon of regret when we knew deep down what we should have done based on our gut feeling, but we ignored it and listened to someone else's advice or opinion.

Your intuition will always lead you to where you need to go and what you should do at any moment in time. It's like a real-time inner GPS that will tell you when to take a detour and which path you should take if there is a blockage in the road to your destination. It's guaranteed that our inner GPS will guide us to exactly where we want to go, but what's not guaranteed is how or which path it will put us on to take us there. There are infinite circumstances that can happen on the journey to the destination, but you can rest assured your GPS will get you there.

Society will almost never confirm our intuition until it's mainstream already. For this reason, if you try to look outside for confirmation on what you know to be true for you, you'll almost always get backlash and differing opinions on what next steps you should take. Avoid looking externally for answers. Follow your intuition, your gut feeling, your inner wisdom, and the Universe/God. When you do this, you will begin to see miracles occurring in your life that you never could have expected or even dreamed of. Those who have the faith and courage to do this, will discover the true joy, peace, and love they have been looking for while enjoying the miracle of life.

HOW DO YOU KNOW WHAT TO DO WITHOUT THINKING? PT.2

The truth is most of us know what to do, but we are just afraid to do it. For instance, if we want to lose weight, most of us know exactly what we need to do. The formula to losing weight isn't rocket science or written in hieroglyphics. Most of us know that all we need to do is burn more calories than we consume, workout and eat healthy foods and we'll lose weight. For anything in life, you most likely already know deep down what to do, but are afraid of doing it or don't believe that you are good enough to do it.

The first step is realizing that you already know what to do, you just think you don't because of fear or self-doubt. If you don't have any fear or self-doubt about the situation and still see that you don't know what to do, then the next step is to trust your inner wisdom (Infinite Intelligence) that it will give you the answers you need. We have the ability to access an infinite number of thoughts, so there's definitely no shortage of ideas on what you can do in any given moment. The only thing that is stopping us from accessing this abundance of knowledge is our own thinking.

Henry Ford once said, "Whether you think that you can or can't, you're right." If we walk around our lives thinking we can't, then we immediately block ourselves from the limitless possibilities of what we can do in any given moment in time. But when we release the brake in our mind and realize that it's just our thinking holding us back, we automatically return to our natural state of abundance and unlimited possibilities and in that moment, we can receive any answer we need on what to do.

In short, know that you already know and if you don't know, know that you can know what you need to know.

If you know that you can always know, then what you need to know will always come to you. Trust in your own intuition and inner wisdom. It has always and will always be there for you when you need it as long as you trust that it will.

HOW TO MAKE DECISIONS THROUGH NON-THINKING

We always intuitively know what to do deep down. It is only when we are clouded with thinking (fear and external influences) that we think we don't know what to do.

Only you know what you truly want and what's most aligned with your soul. No one else can. This process is designed to silence the noise of the external world, let go of thinking, and help you reconnect with your intuition, which always knows what to do and what is most aligned with you.

Your intuition will always take care of you when you trust it. The more you trust your intuition, the more it trusts you.

Your thinking can only think in the past or future, causing anxiety or shame. Your intuition only speaks in the present tense in the moment because it is the only time that actually exists. It can only tell you what the next step for you is and does not worry about the past or future because it knows it is creating both right now.

Your intuition knows this world is truly abundant, so it does not have guilt from the past or anxiety about the future. It knows that unlimited possibilities exists in the present moment and that there are infinite outcomes when you trust it.

Your job is not to try to calculate or control the outcome (thinking), which only causes suffering. Your responsibility is to follow your intuition and to do what you are doing for no other reason than because you love doing it so much.

This is unconditional creation and love, which is abundant by nature. Embodying this energy is what will allow you to attract more in its likeness.

NON-THINKING
DECISION-MAKING GUIDE

Define The Decision

Write down the decision you are trying to make as simply as you can.

Inquire & Let Go By Asking Yourself These Questions

What are you afraid of happening when you make this decision?

Now what are you actually afraid of?

What story is this fear telling you? Write out exactly what it is saying in great detail without filtering anything.

What's the cost of listening to this thinking and fear? List as much as you can out. What is it costing you personally, physically, mentally, emotionally, and spiritually?

Can you see how this is just thinking and how much suffering it is causing you? Do you want to let go of it now?

Remember that thinking is the root cause of suffering. You can choose in this moment to stop believing in it and let go of it to be free.

When you let go of all external opinions, advice, and influences, what do you intuitively know you desire to do? What feels most aligned with you?

How does it feel to follow your intuition?

Write down what your intuition is telling you and what it is inviting you to do right now.

NON-THINKING DECISION-MAKING GUIDE

Define The Decision
Write down the decision you are trying to make as simply as you can.

Inquire & Let Go By Asking Yourself These Questions

What are you afraid of happening when you make this decision?

Now what are you actually afraid of?

What story is this fear telling you? Write out exactly what it is saying in great detail without filtering anything.

What's the cost of listening to this thinking and fear? List as much as you can out. What is it costing you personally, physically, mentally, emotionally, and spiritually?

Can you see how this is just thinking and how much suffering it is causing you? Do you want to let go of it now?

Remember that thinking is the root cause of suffering. You can choose in this moment to stop believing in it and let go of it to be free.

When you let go of all external opinions, advice, and influences, what do you intuitively know you desire to do? What feels most aligned with you?

How does it feel to follow your intuition?

Write down what your intuition is telling you and what it is inviting you to do right now.

NON-THINKING
DECISION-MAKING GUIDE

Define The Decision

Write down the decision you are trying to make as simply as you can.

Inquire & Let Go By Asking Yourself These Questions

What are you afraid of happening when you make this decision?

Now what are you actually afraid of?

What story is this fear telling you? Write out exactly what it is saying in great detail without filtering anything.

What's the cost of listening to this thinking and fear? List as much as you can out. What is it costing you personally, physically, mentally, emotionally, and spiritually?

Can you see how this is just thinking and how much suffering it is causing you? Do you want to let go of it now?

Remember that thinking is the root cause of suffering. You can choose in this moment to stop believing in it and let go of it to be free.

When you let go of all external opinions, advice, and influences, what do you intuitively know you desire to do? What feels most aligned with you?

How does it feel to follow your intuition?

Write down what your intuition is telling you and what it is inviting you to do right now.

NON-THINKING
DECISION-MAKING GUIDE

Define The Decision

Write down the decision you are trying to make as simply as you can.

Inquire & Let Go By Asking Yourself These Questions

What are you afraid of happening when you make this decision?

Now what are you actually afraid of?

What story is this fear telling you? Write out exactly what it is saying in great detail without filtering anything.

What's the cost of listening to this thinking and fear? List as much as you can out. What is it costing you personally, physically, mentally, emotionally, and spiritually?

Can you see how this is just thinking and how much suffering it is causing you?
Do you want to let go of it now?

Remember that thinking is the root cause of suffering. You can choose in this moment to stop believing in it and let go of it to be free.

When you let go of all external opinions, advice, and influences, what do you intuitively know you desire to do? What feels most aligned with you?

How does it feel to follow your intuition?

Write down what your intuition is telling you and what it is inviting you to do right now.

NON-THINKING DECISION-MAKING GUIDE

Define The Decision

Write down the decision you are trying to make as simply as you can.

Inquire & Let Go By Asking Yourself These Questions

What are you afraid of happening when you make this decision?

Now what are you actually afraid of?

What story is this fear telling you? Write out exactly what it is saying in great detail without filtering anything.

What's the cost of listening to this thinking and fear? List as much as you can out. What is it costing you personally, physically, mentally, emotionally, and spiritually?

Can you see how this is just thinking and how much suffering it is causing you?
Do you want to let go of it now?

Remember that thinking is the root cause of suffering. You can choose in this moment to stop believing in it and let go of it to be free.

When you let go of all external opinions, advice, and influences, what do you intuitively know you desire to do? What feels most aligned with you?

How does it feel to follow your intuition?

Write down what your intuition is telling you and what it is inviting you to do right now.

NON-THINKING
DECISION-MAKING GUIDE

Define The Decision
Write down the decision you are trying to make as simply as you can.

Inquire & Let Go By Asking Yourself These Questions

What are you afraid of happening when you make this decision?

Now what are you actually afraid of?

What story is this fear telling you? Write out exactly what it is saying in great detail without filtering anything.

What's the cost of listening to this thinking and fear? List as much as you can out. What is it costing you personally, physically, mentally, emotionally, and spiritually?

Can you see how this is just thinking and how much suffering it is causing you?
Do you want to let go of it now?

Remember that thinking is the root cause of suffering. You can choose in this moment to stop believing in it and let go of it to be free.

When you let go of all external opinions, advice, and influences, what do you intuitively know you desire to do? What feels most aligned with you?

How does it feel to follow your intuition?

Write down what your intuition is telling you and what it is inviting you to do right now.

NON-THINKING
DECISION-MAKING GUIDE

Define The Decision

Write down the decision you are trying to make as simply as you can.

Inquire & Let Go By Asking Yourself These Questions

What are you afraid of happening when you make this decision?

Now what are you actually afraid of?

What story is this fear telling you? Write out exactly what it is saying in great detail without filtering anything.

What's the cost of listening to this thinking and fear? List as much as you can out. What is it costing you personally, physically, mentally, emotionally, and spiritually?

Can you see how this is just thinking and how much suffering it is causing you? Do you want to let go of it now?

Remember that thinking is the root cause of suffering. You can choose in this moment to stop believing in it and let go of it to be free.

When you let go of all external opinions, advice, and influences, what do you intuitively know you desire to do? What feels most aligned with you?

How does it feel to follow your intuition?

Write down what your intuition is telling you and what it is inviting you to do right now.

NON-THINKING
DECISION-MAKING GUIDE

Define The Decision
Write down the decision you are trying to make as simply as you can.

Inquire & Let Go By Asking Yourself These Questions

What are you afraid of happening when you make this decision?

Now what are you actually afraid of?

What story is this fear telling you? Write out exactly what it is saying in great detail without filtering anything.

What's the cost of listening to this thinking and fear? List as much as you can out. What is it costing you personally, physically, mentally, emotionally, and spiritually?

Can you see how this is just thinking and how much suffering it is causing you?
Do you want to let go of it now?

Remember that thinking is the root cause of suffering. You can choose in this moment to stop believing in it and let go of it to be free.

When you let go of all external opinions, advice, and influences, what do you intuitively know you desire to do? What feels most aligned with you?

How does it feel to follow your intuition?

Write down what your intuition is telling you and what it is inviting you to do right now.

NON-THINKING DECISION-MAKING GUIDE

Define The Decision

Write down the decision you are trying to make as simply as you can.

Inquire & Let Go By Asking Yourself These Questions

What are you afraid of happening when you make this decision?

Now what are you actually afraid of?

What story is this fear telling you? Write out exactly what it is saying in great detail without filtering anything.

What's the cost of listening to this thinking and fear? List as much as you can out. What is it costing you personally, physically, mentally, emotionally, and spiritually?

Can you see how this is just thinking and how much suffering it is causing you? Do you want to let go of it now?

Remember that thinking is the root cause of suffering. You can choose in this moment to stop believing in it and let go of it to be free.

When you let go of all external opinions, advice, and influences, what do you intuitively know you desire to do? What feels most aligned with you?

How does it feel to follow your intuition?

Write down what your intuition is telling you and what it is inviting you to do right now.

NON-THINKING
DECISION-MAKING GUIDE

Define The Decision
Write down the decision you are trying to make as simply as you can.

Inquire & Let Go By Asking Yourself These Questions

What are you afraid of happening when you make this decision?

Now what are you actually afraid of?

What story is this fear telling you? Write out exactly what it is saying in great detail without filtering anything.

What's the cost of listening to this thinking and fear? List as much as you can out. What is it costing you personally, physically, mentally, emotionally, and spiritually?

Can you see how this is just thinking and how much suffering it is causing you?
Do you want to let go of it now?

Remember that thinking is the root cause of suffering. You can choose in this moment to stop believing in it and let go of it to be free.

When you let go of all external opinions, advice, and influences, what do you intuitively know you desire to do? What feels most aligned with you?

How does it feel to follow your intuition?

Write down what your intuition is telling you and what it is inviting you to do right now.

NON-THINKING
DECISION-MAKING GUIDE

Define The Decision
Write down the decision you are trying to make as simply as you can.

Inquire & Let Go By Asking Yourself These Questions

What are you afraid of happening when you make this decision?

Now what are you actually afraid of?

What story is this fear telling you? Write out exactly what it is saying in great detail without filtering anything.

What's the cost of listening to this thinking and fear? List as much as you can out. What is it costing you personally, physically, mentally, emotionally, and spiritually?

Can you see how this is just thinking and how much suffering it is causing you? Do you want to let go of it now?

Remember that thinking is the root cause of suffering. You can choose in this moment to stop believing in it and let go of it to be free.

When you let go of all external opinions, advice, and influences, what do you intuitively know you desire to do? What feels most aligned with you?

How does it feel to follow your intuition?

Write down what your intuition is telling you and what it is inviting you to do right now.

NON-THINKING
DECISION-MAKING GUIDE

Define The Decision
Write down the decision you are trying to make as simply as you can.

Inquire & Let Go By Asking Yourself These Questions

What are you afraid of happening when you make this decision?

Now what are you actually afraid of?

What story is this fear telling you? Write out exactly what it is saying in great detail without filtering anything.

What's the cost of listening to this thinking and fear? List as much as you can out. What is it costing you personally, physically, mentally, emotionally, and spiritually?

Can you see how this is just thinking and how much suffering it is causing you?
Do you want to let go of it now?

Remember that thinking is the root cause of suffering. You can choose in this moment to stop believing in it and let go of it to be free.

When you let go of all external opinions, advice, and influences, what do you intuitively know you desire to do? What feels most aligned with you?

How does it feel to follow your intuition?

Write down what your intuition is telling you and what it is inviting you to do right now.

NON-THINKING
DECISION-MAKING GUIDE

Define The Decision
Write down the decision you are trying to make as simply as you can.

Inquire & Let Go By Asking Yourself These Questions

What are you afraid of happening when you make this decision?

Now what are you actually afraid of?

What story is this fear telling you? Write out exactly what it is saying in great detail without filtering anything.

What's the cost of listening to this thinking and fear? List as much as you can out. What is it costing you personally, physically, mentally, emotionally, and spiritually?

Can you see how this is just thinking and how much suffering it is causing you? Do you want to let go of it now?

Remember that thinking is the root cause of suffering. You can choose in this moment to stop believing in it and let go of it to be free.

When you let go of all external opinions, advice, and influences, what do you intuitively know you desire to do? What feels most aligned with you?

How does it feel to follow your intuition?

Write down what your intuition is telling you and what it is inviting you to do right now.

NON-THINKING DECISION-MAKING GUIDE

Define The Decision

Write down the decision you are trying to make as simply as you can.

Inquire & Let Go By Asking Yourself These Questions

What are you afraid of happening when you make this decision?

Now what are you actually afraid of?

What story is this fear telling you? Write out exactly what it is saying in great detail without filtering anything.

What's the cost of listening to this thinking and fear? List as much as you can out. What is it costing you personally, physically, mentally, emotionally, and spiritually?

Can you see how this is just thinking and how much suffering it is causing you?
Do you want to let go of it now?

Remember that thinking is the root cause of suffering. You can choose in this moment to stop believing in it and let go of it to be free.

When you let go of all external opinions, advice, and influences, what do you intuitively know you desire to do? What feels most aligned with you?

How does it feel to follow your intuition?

Write down what your intuition is telling you and what it is inviting you to do right now.

NON-THINKING DECISION-MAKING GUIDE

Define The Decision
Write down the decision you are trying to make as simply as you can.

Inquire & Let Go By Asking Yourself These Questions

What are you afraid of happening when you make this decision?

Now what are you actually afraid of?

What story is this fear telling you? Write out exactly what it is saying in great detail without filtering anything.

What's the cost of listening to this thinking and fear? List as much as you can out. What is it costing you personally, physically, mentally, emotionally, and spiritually?

Can you see how this is just thinking and how much suffering it is causing you?
Do you want to let go of it now?

Remember that thinking is the root cause of suffering. You can choose in this moment to stop believing in it and let go of it to be free.

When you let go of all external opinions, advice, and influences, what do you intuitively know you desire to do? What feels most aligned with you?

How does it feel to follow your intuition?

Write down what your intuition is telling you and what it is inviting you to do right now.

NON-THINKING
DECISION-MAKING GUIDE

Define The Decision
Write down the decision you are trying to make as simply as you can.

Inquire & Let Go By Asking Yourself These Questions

What are you afraid of happening when you make this decision?

Now what are you actually afraid of?

What story is this fear telling you? Write out exactly what it is saying in great detail without filtering anything.

What's the cost of listening to this thinking and fear? List as much as you can out. What is it costing you personally, physically, mentally, emotionally, and spiritually?

Can you see how this is just thinking and how much suffering it is causing you?
Do you want to let go of it now?

Remember that thinking is the root cause of suffering. You can choose in this moment to stop believing in it and let go of it to be free.

When you let go of all external opinions, advice, and influences, what do you intuitively know you desire to do? What feels most aligned with you?

How does it feel to follow your intuition?

Write down what your intuition is telling you and what it is inviting you to do right now.

NON-THINKING
DECISION-MAKING GUIDE

Define The Decision

Write down the decision you are trying to make as simply as you can.

Inquire & Let Go By Asking Yourself These Questions

What are you afraid of happening when you make this decision?

Now what are you actually afraid of?

What story is this fear telling you? Write out exactly what it is saying in great detail without filtering anything.

What's the cost of listening to this thinking and fear? List as much as you can out. What is it costing you personally, physically, mentally, emotionally, and spiritually?

Can you see how this is just thinking and how much suffering it is causing you?
Do you want to let go of it now?

Remember that thinking is the root cause of suffering. You can choose in this moment to stop believing in it and let go of it to be free.

When you let go of all external opinions, advice, and influences, what do you intuitively know you desire to do? What feels most aligned with you?

How does it feel to follow your intuition?

Write down what your intuition is telling you and what it is inviting you to do right now.

NON-THINKING
DECISION-MAKING GUIDE

Define The Decision
Write down the decision you are trying to make as simply as you can.

Inquire & Let Go By Asking Yourself These Questions

What are you afraid of happening when you make this decision?

Now what are you actually afraid of?

What story is this fear telling you? Write out exactly what it is saying in great detail without filtering anything.

What's the cost of listening to this thinking and fear? List as much as you can out. What is it costing you personally, physically, mentally, emotionally, and spiritually?

Can you see how this is just thinking and how much suffering it is causing you?
Do you want to let go of it now?

Remember that thinking is the root cause of suffering. You can choose in this moment to stop believing in it and let go of it to be free.

When you let go of all external opinions, advice, and influences, what do you intuitively know you desire to do? What feels most aligned with you?

How does it feel to follow your intuition?

Write down what your intuition is telling you and what it is inviting you to do right now.

NON-THINKING
DECISION-MAKING GUIDE

Define The Decision

Write down the decision you are trying to make as simply as you can.

Inquire & Let Go By Asking Yourself These Questions

What are you afraid of happening when you make this decision?

Now what are you actually afraid of?

What story is this fear telling you? Write out exactly what it is saying in great detail without filtering anything.

What's the cost of listening to this thinking and fear? List as much as you can out. What is it costing you personally, physically, mentally, emotionally, and spiritually?

Can you see how this is just thinking and how much suffering it is causing you?
Do you want to let go of it now?

Remember that thinking is the root cause of suffering. You can choose in this moment to stop believing in it and let go of it to be free.

When you let go of all external opinions, advice, and influences, what do you intuitively know you desire to do? What feels most aligned with you?

How does it feel to follow your intuition?

Write down what your intuition is telling you and what it is inviting you to do right now.

NON-THINKING DECISION-MAKING GUIDE

Define The Decision

Write down the decision you are trying to make as simply as you can.

Inquire & Let Go By Asking Yourself These Questions

What are you afraid of happening when you make this decision?

Now what are you actually afraid of?

What story is this fear telling you? Write out exactly what it is saying in great detail without filtering anything.

What's the cost of listening to this thinking and fear? List as much as you can out. What is it costing you personally, physically, mentally, emotionally, and spiritually?

Can you see how this is just thinking and how much suffering it is causing you?
Do you want to let go of it now?

Remember that thinking is the root cause of suffering. You can choose in this moment to stop believing in it and let go of it to be free.

When you let go of all external opinions, advice, and influences, what do you intuitively know you desire to do? What feels most aligned with you?

How does it feel to follow your intuition?

Write down what your intuition is telling you and what it is inviting you to do right now.

NON-THINKING
DECISION-MAKING GUIDE

Define The Decision
Write down the decision you are trying to make as simply as you can.

Inquire & Let Go By Asking Yourself These Questions

What are you afraid of happening when you make this decision?

Now what are you actually afraid of?

What story is this fear telling you? Write out exactly what it is saying in great detail without filtering anything.

What's the cost of listening to this thinking and fear? List as much as you can out. What is it costing you personally, physically, mentally, emotionally, and spiritually?

Can you see how this is just thinking and how much suffering it is causing you? Do you want to let go of it now?

Remember that thinking is the root cause of suffering. You can choose in this moment to stop believing in it and let go of it to be free.

When you let go of all external opinions, advice, and influences, what do you intuitively know you desire to do? What feels most aligned with you?

How does it feel to follow your intuition?

Write down what your intuition is telling you and what it is inviting you to do right now.

NON-THINKING DECISION-MAKING GUIDE

Define The Decision

Write down the decision you are trying to make as simply as you can.

Inquire & Let Go By Asking Yourself These Questions

What are you afraid of happening when you make this decision?

Now what are you actually afraid of?

What story is this fear telling you? Write out exactly what it is saying in great detail without filtering anything.

What's the cost of listening to this thinking and fear? List as much as you can out. What is it costing you personally, physically, mentally, emotionally, and spiritually?

Can you see how this is just thinking and how much suffering it is causing you?
Do you want to let go of it now?

Remember that thinking is the root cause of suffering. You can choose in this moment to stop believing in it and let go of it to be free.

When you let go of all external opinions, advice, and influences, what do you intuitively know you desire to do? What feels most aligned with you?

How does it feel to follow your intuition?

Write down what your intuition is telling you and what it is inviting you to do right now.

NON-THINKING DECISION-MAKING GUIDE

Define The Decision

Write down the decision you are trying to make as simply as you can.

Inquire & Let Go By Asking Yourself These Questions

What are you afraid of happening when you make this decision?

Now what are you actually afraid of?

What story is this fear telling you? Write out exactly what it is saying in great detail without filtering anything.

What's the cost of listening to this thinking and fear? List as much as you can out. What is it costing you personally, physically, mentally, emotionally, and spiritually?

Can you see how this is just thinking and how much suffering it is causing you?
Do you want to let go of it now?

Remember that thinking is the root cause of suffering. You can choose in this moment to stop believing in it and let go of it to be free.

When you let go of all external opinions, advice, and influences, what do you intuitively know you desire to do? What feels most aligned with you?

How does it feel to follow your intuition?

Write down what your intuition is telling you and what it is inviting you to do right now.

NON-THINKING DECISION-MAKING GUIDE

Define The Decision

Write down the decision you are trying to make as simply as you can.

Inquire & Let Go By Asking Yourself These Questions

What are you afraid of happening when you make this decision?

Now what are you actually afraid of?

What story is this fear telling you? Write out exactly what it is saying in great detail without filtering anything.

What's the cost of listening to this thinking and fear? List as much as you can out. What is it costing you personally, physically, mentally, emotionally, and spiritually?

Can you see how this is just thinking and how much suffering it is causing you? Do you want to let go of it now?

Remember that thinking is the root cause of suffering. You can choose in this moment to stop believing in it and let go of it to be free.

When you let go of all external opinions, advice, and influences, what do you intuitively know you desire to do? What feels most aligned with you?

How does it feel to follow your intuition?

Write down what your intuition is telling you and what it is inviting you to do right now.

NON-THINKING DECISION-MAKING GUIDE

Define The Decision

Write down the decision you are trying to make as simply as you can.

Inquire & Let Go By Asking Yourself These Questions

What are you afraid of happening when you make this decision?

Now what are you actually afraid of?

What story is this fear telling you? Write out exactly what it is saying in great detail without filtering anything.

What's the cost of listening to this thinking and fear? List as much as you can out. What is it costing you personally, physically, mentally, emotionally, and spiritually?

Can you see how this is just thinking and how much suffering it is causing you? Do you want to let go of it now?

Remember that thinking is the root cause of suffering. You can choose in this moment to stop believing in it and let go of it to be free.

When you let go of all external opinions, advice, and influences, what do you intuitively know you desire to do? What feels most aligned with you?

How does it feel to follow your intuition?

Write down what your intuition is telling you and what it is inviting you to do right now.

THE FEAR NEUTRALIZATION PROCESS

The only thing stopping us from doing what we truly desire in this world and following our intuition is fear, which is created from our thinking. This is why thinking is the root cause of all psychological and emotional suffering.

We are not afraid of what we think we are afraid of (external things). We are afraid of how we think we'll feel if it happens. Fear is internal, not external. This is great news because we can always change and let go of what is internal.

The process of overcoming fear is through questioning what it is you are truly afraid of and then seeing the truth behind this fear. It is only when we see what is actually happening in our minds that we can let go of it to be free.

Most of the time we feel fear and just suppress or avoid the fear, which only magnifies it and allows it to control you more.

When we are able to have the courage to examine our fears and look at the truth beyond our thinking, the illusion of the fear dissolves and we fall back into peace. In this state of non-thinking, a state of pure presence and complete peace, we always know what to do and may move towards it without anything holding us back any longer.

THE FEAR NEUTRALIZATION GUIDE

Define The Fear

What are you afraid of? Be short and specific.

Inquire & Examine What's Behind Your Thinking

Take a closer look at the fear. You're not afraid of it happening. You're afraid of how you'll feel if it happens. What are you afraid of feeling?

What conclusion have you made about yourself if what you're afraid of happens? Example of a conclusion: If (insert what you're afraid of happening or doing) then it means I'm (insert conclusion)

What does this conclusion even mean?

Does this conclusion (thinking) feel heavy and draining or light and expansive?

What is it costing you to continue believing this thinking (conclusion)?
Write down as much as you can here and really feel it.

Can you see how this conclusion (which comes from thinking) created a condition that causes you suffering?

Are you ready to stop believing in this thinking and let go of it?

How does it feel when you visualize letting it go?

What is your intuition telling you right now?

How does your intuition feel in comparison to your thinking?

Set an intention to follow your intuition and follow it now.

THE FEAR NEUTRALIZATION GUIDE

Define The Fear

What are you afraid of? Be short and specific.

Inquire & Examine What's Behind Your Thinking

Take a closer look at the fear. You're not afraid of it happening. You're afraid of how you'll feel if it happens. What are you afraid of feeling?

What conclusion have you made about yourself if what you're afraid of happens? Example of a conclusion: If (insert what you're afraid of happening or doing) then it means I'm (insert conclusion)

What does this conclusion even mean?

Does this conclusion (thinking) feel heavy and draining or light and expansive?

What is it costing you to continue believing this thinking (conclusion)?
Write down as much as you can here and really feel it.

Can you see how this conclusion (which comes from thinking) created a condition that causes you suffering?

Are you ready to stop believing in this thinking and let go of it?

How does it feel when you visualize letting it go?

What is your intuition telling you right now?

How does your intuition feel in comparison to your thinking?

Set an intention to follow your intuition and follow it now.

THE FEAR
NEUTRALIZATION GUIDE

Define The Fear

What are you afraid of? Be short and specific.

Inquire & Examine What's Behind Your Thinking

Take a closer look at the fear. You're not afraid of it happening. You're afraid of how you'll feel if it happens. What are you afraid of feeling?

What conclusion have you made about yourself if what you're afraid of happens? Example of a conclusion: If (insert what you're afraid of happening or doing) then it means I'm (insert conclusion)

What does this conclusion even mean?

Does this conclusion (thinking) feel heavy and draining or light and expansive?

What is it costing you to continue believing this thinking (conclusion)?
Write down as much as you can here and really feel it.

Can you see how this conclusion (which comes from thinking) created a condition that causes you suffering?

Are you ready to stop believing in this thinking and let go of it?

How does it feel when you visualize letting it go?

What is your intuition telling you right now?

How does your intuition feel in comparison to your thinking?

Set an intention to follow your intuition and follow it now.

THE FEAR
NEUTRALIZATION GUIDE

Define The Fear
What are you afraid of? Be short and specific.

Inquire & Examine What's Behind Your Thinking
Take a closer look at the fear. You're not afraid of it happening. You're afraid of how you'll feel if it happens. What are you afraid of feeling?

What conclusion have you made about yourself if what you're afraid of happens? Example of a conclusion: If (insert what you're afraid of happening or doing) then it means I'm (insert conclusion)

What does this conclusion even mean?

Does this conclusion (thinking) feel heavy and draining or light and expansive?

What is it costing you to continue believing this thinking (conclusion)?
Write down as much as you can here and really feel it.

Can you see how this conclusion (which comes from thinking) created a condition that causes you suffering?

Are you ready to stop believing in this thinking and let go of it?

How does it feel when you visualize letting it go?

What is your intuition telling you right now?

How does your intuition feel in comparison to your thinking?

Set an intention to follow your intuition and follow it now.

THE FEAR NEUTRALIZATION GUIDE

Define The Fear
What are you afraid of? Be short and specific.

Inquire & Examine What's Behind Your Thinking
Take a closer look at the fear. You're not afraid of it happening. You're afraid of how you'll feel if it happens. What are you afraid of feeling?

What conclusion have you made about yourself if what you're afraid of happens? Example of a conclusion: If (insert what you're afraid of happening or doing) then it means I'm (insert conclusion)

What does this conclusion even mean?

Does this conclusion (thinking) feel heavy and draining or light and expansive?

What is it costing you to continue believing this thinking (conclusion)?
Write down as much as you can here and really feel it.

Can you see how this conclusion (which comes from thinking) created a condition that causes you suffering?

Are you ready to stop believing in this thinking and let go of it?

How does it feel when you visualize letting it go?

What is your intuition telling you right now?

How does your intuition feel in comparison to your thinking?

Set an intention to follow your intuition and follow it now.

THE FEAR
NEUTRALIZATION GUIDE

Define The Fear
What are you afraid of? Be short and specific.

Inquire & Examine What's Behind Your Thinking
Take a closer look at the fear. You're not afraid of it happening. You're afraid of how you'll feel if it happens. What are you afraid of feeling?

What conclusion have you made about yourself if what you're afraid of happens? Example of a conclusion: If (insert what you're afraid of happening or doing) then it means I'm (insert conclusion)

What does this conclusion even mean?

Does this conclusion (thinking) feel heavy and draining or light and expansive?

What is it costing you to continue believing this thinking (conclusion)?
Write down as much as you can here and really feel it.

Can you see how this conclusion (which comes from thinking) created a condition that causes you suffering?

Are you ready to stop believing in this thinking and let go of it?

How does it feel when you visualize letting it go?

What is your intuition telling you right now?

How does your intuition feel in comparison to your thinking?

Set an intention to follow your intuition and follow it now.

THE FEAR
NEUTRALIZATION GUIDE

Define The Fear

What are you afraid of? Be short and specific.

Inquire & Examine What's Behind Your Thinking

Take a closer look at the fear. You're not afraid of it happening. You're afraid of how you'll feel if it happens. What are you afraid of feeling?

What conclusion have you made about yourself if what you're afraid of happens? Example of a conclusion: If (insert what you're afraid of happening or doing) then it means I'm (insert conclusion)

What does this conclusion even mean?

Does this conclusion (thinking) feel heavy and draining or light and expansive?

What is it costing you to continue believing this thinking (conclusion)?
Write down as much as you can here and really feel it.

Can you see how this conclusion (which comes from thinking) created a condition that causes you suffering?

Are you ready to stop believing in this thinking and let go of it?

How does it feel when you visualize letting it go?

What is your intuition telling you right now?

How does your intuition feel in comparison to your thinking?

Set an intention to follow your intuition and follow it now.

THE FEAR NEUTRALIZATION GUIDE

Define The Fear

What are you afraid of? Be short and specific.

Inquire & Examine What's Behind Your Thinking

Take a closer look at the fear. You're not afraid of it happening. You're afraid of how you'll feel if it happens. What are you afraid of feeling?

What conclusion have you made about yourself if what you're afraid of happens? Example of a conclusion: If (insert what you're afraid of happening or doing) then it means I'm (insert conclusion)

What does this conclusion even mean?

Does this conclusion (thinking) feel heavy and draining or light and expansive?

What is it costing you to continue believing this thinking (conclusion)?
Write down as much as you can here and really feel it.

Can you see how this conclusion (which comes from thinking) created a condition that causes you suffering?

Are you ready to stop believing in this thinking and let go of it?

How does it feel when you visualize letting it go?

What is your intuition telling you right now?

How does your intuition feel in comparison to your thinking?

Set an intention to follow your intuition and follow it now.

THE FEAR
NEUTRALIZATION GUIDE

Define The Fear
What are you afraid of? Be short and specific.

Inquire & Examine What's Behind Your Thinking
Take a closer look at the fear. You're not afraid of it happening. You're afraid of how you'll feel if it happens. What are you afraid of feeling?

What conclusion have you made about yourself if what you're afraid of happens? Example of a conclusion: If (insert what you're afraid of happening or doing) then it means I'm (insert conclusion)

What does this conclusion even mean?

Does this conclusion (thinking) feel heavy and draining or light and expansive?

What is it costing you to continue believing this thinking (conclusion)?
Write down as much as you can here and really feel it.

Can you see how this conclusion (which comes from thinking) created a condition that causes you suffering?

Are you ready to stop believing in this thinking and let go of it?

How does it feel when you visualize letting it go?

What is your intuition telling you right now?

How does your intuition feel in comparison to your thinking?

Set an intention to follow your intuition and follow it now.

THE FEAR
NEUTRALIZATION GUIDE

Define The Fear

What are you afraid of? Be short and specific.

Inquire & Examine What's Behind Your Thinking

Take a closer look at the fear. You're not afraid of it happening. You're afraid of how you'll feel if it happens. What are you afraid of feeling?

What conclusion have you made about yourself if what you're afraid of happens? Example of a conclusion: If (insert what you're afraid of happening or doing) then it means I'm (insert conclusion)

What does this conclusion even mean?

Does this conclusion (thinking) feel heavy and draining or light and expansive?

What is it costing you to continue believing this thinking (conclusion)?
Write down as much as you can here and really feel it.

Can you see how this conclusion (which comes from thinking) created a condition that causes you suffering?

Are you ready to stop believing in this thinking and let go of it?

How does it feel when you visualize letting it go?

What is your intuition telling you right now?

How does your intuition feel in comparison to your thinking?

Set an intention to follow your intuition and follow it now.

THE FEAR
NEUTRALIZATION GUIDE

Define The Fear
What are you afraid of? Be short and specific.

Inquire & Examine What's Behind Your Thinking
Take a closer look at the fear. You're not afraid of it happening. You're afraid of how you'll feel if it happens. What are you afraid of feeling?

What conclusion have you made about yourself if what you're afraid of happens? Example of a conclusion: If (insert what you're afraid of happening or doing) then it means I'm (insert conclusion)

What does this conclusion even mean?

Does this conclusion (thinking) feel heavy and draining or light and expansive?

What is it costing you to continue believing this thinking (conclusion)?
Write down as much as you can here and really feel it.

Can you see how this conclusion (which comes from thinking) created a condition that causes you suffering?

Are you ready to stop believing in this thinking and let go of it?

How does it feel when you visualize letting it go?

What is your intuition telling you right now?

How does your intuition feel in comparison to your thinking?

Set an intention to follow your intuition and follow it now.

THE FEAR
NEUTRALIZATION GUIDE

Define The Fear
What are you afraid of? Be short and specific.

Inquire & Examine What's Behind Your Thinking
Take a closer look at the fear. You're not afraid of it happening. You're afraid of how you'll feel if it happens. What are you afraid of feeling?

What conclusion have you made about yourself if what you're afraid of happens? Example of a conclusion: If (insert what you're afraid of happening or doing) then it means I'm (insert conclusion)

What does this conclusion even mean?

Does this conclusion (thinking) feel heavy and draining or light and expansive?

What is it costing you to continue believing this thinking (conclusion)?
Write down as much as you can here and really feel it.

Can you see how this conclusion (which comes from thinking) created a condition that causes you suffering?

Are you ready to stop believing in this thinking and let go of it?

How does it feel when you visualize letting it go?

What is your intuition telling you right now?

How does your intuition feel in comparison to your thinking?

Set an intention to follow your intuition and follow it now.

THE FEAR NEUTRALIZATION GUIDE

Define The Fear
What are you afraid of? Be short and specific.

Inquire & Examine What's Behind Your Thinking
Take a closer look at the fear. You're not afraid of it happening. You're afraid of how you'll feel if it happens. What are you afraid of feeling?

What conclusion have you made about yourself if what you're afraid of happens? Example of a conclusion: If (insert what you're afraid of happening or doing) then it means I'm (insert conclusion)

What does this conclusion even mean?

Does this conclusion (thinking) feel heavy and draining or light and expansive?

What is it costing you to continue believing this thinking (conclusion)?
Write down as much as you can here and really feel it.

Can you see how this conclusion (which comes from thinking) created a condition that causes you suffering?

Are you ready to stop believing in this thinking and let go of it?

How does it feel when you visualize letting it go?

What is your intuition telling you right now?

How does your intuition feel in comparison to your thinking?

Set an intention to follow your intuition and follow it now.

THE FEAR NEUTRALIZATION GUIDE

Define The Fear

What are you afraid of? Be short and specific.

Inquire & Examine What's Behind Your Thinking

Take a closer look at the fear. You're not afraid of it happening. You're afraid of how you'll feel if it happens. What are you afraid of feeling?

What conclusion have you made about yourself if what you're afraid of happens? Example of a conclusion: If (insert what you're afraid of happening or doing) then it means I'm (insert conclusion)

What does this conclusion even mean?

Does this conclusion (thinking) feel heavy and draining or light and expansive?

What is it costing you to continue believing this thinking (conclusion)?
Write down as much as you can here and really feel it.

Can you see how this conclusion (which comes from thinking) created a condition that causes you suffering?

Are you ready to stop believing in this thinking and let go of it?

How does it feel when you visualize letting it go?

What is your intuition telling you right now?

How does your intuition feel in comparison to your thinking?

Set an intention to follow your intuition and follow it now.

THE FEAR NEUTRALIZATION GUIDE

Define The Fear

What are you afraid of? Be short and specific.

Inquire & Examine What's Behind Your Thinking

Take a closer look at the fear. You're not afraid of it happening. You're afraid of how you'll feel if it happens. What are you afraid of feeling?

What conclusion have you made about yourself if what you're afraid of happens? Example of a conclusion: If (insert what you're afraid of happening or doing) then it means I'm (insert conclusion)

What does this conclusion even mean?

Does this conclusion (thinking) feel heavy and draining or light and expansive?

What is it costing you to continue believing this thinking (conclusion)?
Write down as much as you can here and really feel it.

Can you see how this conclusion (which comes from thinking) created a condition that causes you suffering?

Are you ready to stop believing in this thinking and let go of it?

How does it feel when you visualize letting it go?

What is your intuition telling you right now?

How does your intuition feel in comparison to your thinking?

Set an intention to follow your intuition and follow it now.

THE FEAR
NEUTRALIZATION GUIDE

Define The Fear
What are you afraid of? Be short and specific.

Inquire & Examine What's Behind Your Thinking
Take a closer look at the fear. You're not afraid of it happening. You're afraid of how you'll feel if it happens. What are you afraid of feeling?

What conclusion have you made about yourself if what you're afraid of happens? Example of a conclusion: If (insert what you're afraid of happening or doing) then it means I'm (insert conclusion)

What does this conclusion even mean?

Does this conclusion (thinking) feel heavy and draining or light and expansive?

What is it costing you to continue believing this thinking (conclusion)?
Write down as much as you can here and really feel it.

Can you see how this conclusion (which comes from thinking) created a condition that causes you suffering?

Are you ready to stop believing in this thinking and let go of it?

How does it feel when you visualize letting it go?

What is your intuition telling you right now?

How does your intuition feel in comparison to your thinking?

Set an intention to follow your intuition and follow it now.

THE FEAR
NEUTRALIZATION GUIDE

Define The Fear
What are you afraid of? Be short and specific.

Inquire & Examine What's Behind Your Thinking
Take a closer look at the fear. You're not afraid of it happening. You're afraid of how you'll feel if it happens. What are you afraid of feeling?

What conclusion have you made about yourself if what you're afraid of happens? Example of a conclusion: If (insert what you're afraid of happening or doing) then it means I'm (insert conclusion)

What does this conclusion even mean?

Does this conclusion (thinking) feel heavy and draining or light and expansive?

What is it costing you to continue believing this thinking (conclusion)?
Write down as much as you can here and really feel it.

Can you see how this conclusion (which comes from thinking) created a condition that causes you suffering?

Are you ready to stop believing in this thinking and let go of it?

How does it feel when you visualize letting it go?

What is your intuition telling you right now?

How does your intuition feel in comparison to your thinking?

Set an intention to follow your intuition and follow it now.

THE FEAR
NEUTRALIZATION GUIDE

Define The Fear

What are you afraid of? Be short and specific.

Inquire & Examine What's Behind Your Thinking

Take a closer look at the fear. You're not afraid of it happening. You're afraid of how you'll feel if it happens. What are you afraid of feeling?

What conclusion have you made about yourself if what you're afraid of happens? Example of a conclusion: If (insert what you're afraid of happening or doing) then it means I'm (insert conclusion)

What does this conclusion even mean?

Does this conclusion (thinking) feel heavy and draining or light and expansive?

What is it costing you to continue believing this thinking (conclusion)?
Write down as much as you can here and really feel it.

Can you see how this conclusion (which comes from thinking) created a condition that causes you suffering?

Are you ready to stop believing in this thinking and let go of it?

How does it feel when you visualize letting it go?

What is your intuition telling you right now?

How does your intuition feel in comparison to your thinking?

Set an intention to follow your intuition and follow it now.

THE FEAR
NEUTRALIZATION GUIDE

Define The Fear
What are you afraid of? Be short and specific.

Inquire & Examine What's Behind Your Thinking
Take a closer look at the fear. You're not afraid of it happening. You're afraid of how you'll feel if it happens. What are you afraid of feeling?

What conclusion have you made about yourself if what you're afraid of happens? Example of a conclusion: If (insert what you're afraid of happening or doing) then it means I'm (insert conclusion)

What does this conclusion even mean?

Does this conclusion (thinking) feel heavy and draining or light and expansive?

What is it costing you to continue believing this thinking (conclusion)?
Write down as much as you can here and really feel it.

Can you see how this conclusion (which comes from thinking) created a condition that causes you suffering?

Are you ready to stop believing in this thinking and let go of it?

How does it feel when you visualize letting it go?

What is your intuition telling you right now?

How does your intuition feel in comparison to your thinking?

Set an intention to follow your intuition and follow it now.

THE FEAR NEUTRALIZATION GUIDE

Define The Fear

What are you afraid of? Be short and specific.

Inquire & Examine What's Behind Your Thinking

Take a closer look at the fear. You're not afraid of it happening. You're afraid of how you'll feel if it happens. What are you afraid of feeling?

What conclusion have you made about yourself if what you're afraid of happens? Example of a conclusion: If (insert what you're afraid of happening or doing) then it means I'm (insert conclusion)

What does this conclusion even mean?

Does this conclusion (thinking) feel heavy and draining or light and expansive?

What is it costing you to continue believing this thinking (conclusion)?
Write down as much as you can here and really feel it.

Can you see how this conclusion (which comes from thinking) created a condition that causes you suffering?

Are you ready to stop believing in this thinking and let go of it?

How does it feel when you visualize letting it go?

What is your intuition telling you right now?

How does your intuition feel in comparison to your thinking?

Set an intention to follow your intuition and follow it now.

THE FEAR NEUTRALIZATION GUIDE

Define The Fear

What are you afraid of? Be short and specific.

Inquire & Examine What's Behind Your Thinking

Take a closer look at the fear. You're not afraid of it happening. You're afraid of how you'll feel if it happens. What are you afraid of feeling?

What conclusion have you made about yourself if what you're afraid of happens? Example of a conclusion: If (insert what you're afraid of happening or doing) then it means I'm (insert conclusion)

What does this conclusion even mean?

Does this conclusion (thinking) feel heavy and draining or light and expansive?

What is it costing you to continue believing this thinking (conclusion)?
Write down as much as you can here and really feel it.

Can you see how this conclusion (which comes from thinking) created a condition that causes you suffering?

Are you ready to stop believing in this thinking and let go of it?

How does it feel when you visualize letting it go?

What is your intuition telling you right now?

How does your intuition feel in comparison to your thinking?

Set an intention to follow your intuition and follow it now.

THE FEAR
NEUTRALIZATION GUIDE

Define The Fear

What are you afraid of? Be short and specific.

Inquire & Examine What's Behind Your Thinking

Take a closer look at the fear. You're not afraid of it happening. You're afraid of how you'll feel if it happens. What are you afraid of feeling?

What conclusion have you made about yourself if what you're afraid of happens? Example of a conclusion: If (insert what you're afraid of happening or doing) then it means I'm (insert conclusion)

What does this conclusion even mean?

Does this conclusion (thinking) feel heavy and draining or light and expansive?

What is it costing you to continue believing this thinking (conclusion)?
Write down as much as you can here and really feel it.

Can you see how this conclusion (which comes from thinking) created a condition that causes you suffering?

Are you ready to stop believing in this thinking and let go of it?

How does it feel when you visualize letting it go?

What is your intuition telling you right now?

How does your intuition feel in comparison to your thinking?

Set an intention to follow your intuition and follow it now.

THE FEAR
NEUTRALIZATION GUIDE

Define The Fear

What are you afraid of? Be short and specific.

Inquire & Examine What's Behind Your Thinking

Take a closer look at the fear. You're not afraid of it happening. You're afraid of how you'll feel if it happens. What are you afraid of feeling?

What conclusion have you made about yourself if what you're afraid of happens? Example of a conclusion: If (insert what you're afraid of happening or doing) then it means I'm (insert conclusion)

What does this conclusion even mean?

Does this conclusion (thinking) feel heavy and draining or light and expansive?

What is it costing you to continue believing this thinking (conclusion)?
Write down as much as you can here and really feel it.

Can you see how this conclusion (which comes from thinking) created a condition that causes you suffering?

Are you ready to stop believing in this thinking and let go of it?

How does it feel when you visualize letting it go?

What is your intuition telling you right now?

How does your intuition feel in comparison to your thinking?

Set an intention to follow your intuition and follow it now.

THE FEAR NEUTRALIZATION GUIDE

Define The Fear

What are you afraid of? Be short and specific.

Inquire & Examine What's Behind Your Thinking

Take a closer look at the fear. You're not afraid of it happening. You're afraid of how you'll feel if it happens. What are you afraid of feeling?

What conclusion have you made about yourself if what you're afraid of happens? Example of a conclusion: If (insert what you're afraid of happening or doing) then it means I'm (insert conclusion)

What does this conclusion even mean?

Does this conclusion (thinking) feel heavy and draining or light and expansive?

What is it costing you to continue believing this thinking (conclusion)?
Write down as much as you can here and really feel it.

Can you see how this conclusion (which comes from thinking) created a condition that causes you suffering?

Are you ready to stop believing in this thinking and let go of it?

How does it feel when you visualize letting it go?

What is your intuition telling you right now?

How does your intuition feel in comparison to your thinking?

Set an intention to follow your intuition and follow it now.

THE FEAR NEUTRALIZATION GUIDE

Define The Fear

What are you afraid of? Be short and specific.

Inquire & Examine What's Behind Your Thinking

Take a closer look at the fear. You're not afraid of it happening. You're afraid of how you'll feel if it happens. What are you afraid of feeling?

What conclusion have you made about yourself if what you're afraid of happens? Example of a conclusion: If (insert what you're afraid of happening or doing) then it means I'm (insert conclusion)

What does this conclusion even mean?

Does this conclusion (thinking) feel heavy and draining or light and expansive?

What is it costing you to continue believing this thinking (conclusion)?
Write down as much as you can here and really feel it.

Can you see how this conclusion (which comes from thinking) created a condition that causes you suffering?

Are you ready to stop believing in this thinking and let go of it?

How does it feel when you visualize letting it go?

What is your intuition telling you right now?

How does your intuition feel in comparison to your thinking?

Set an intention to follow your intuition and follow it now.

EXTERNAL INTEGRATION GUIDES

The first few guides you went through were created to help you end suffering and support you in mastering your inner world to find peace within. Now it is time to design an expansive and peaceful outer environment that will help you stay aligned with your true self through these 'External Integration Guides'.

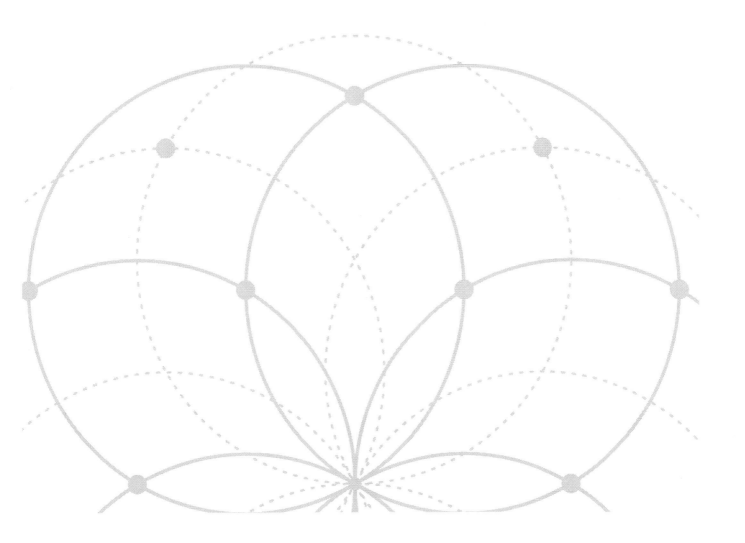

DESIGNING A NON-THINKING ENVIRONMENT

Introduction

Your environment will either induce and support the state of non-thinking or it can make you more prone to thinking.

Although we create our reality from the inside-out, many times we are still affected by our environment. Since we are spiritual beings living in a physical world, we cannot completely detach from this 3D world just yet, so it is important to create an environment that is conducive to non-thinking. In order to be productive, the best way to do it is to eliminate distractions instead of trying to do more.

Similarly, if we eliminate many of the things that we know that can trigger us to relapse back into thinking, then we will be able to stay in a peaceful state of non-thinking much easier. Remember that changing your environment and not yourself will not work long term. A delicate blend of both will be what you need to create a beautiful life you love to live.

NON-THINKING FRAMEWORK

REMOVING THINKING TRIGGERS

Step 1: Perform an audit to see what things can make you more susceptible to thinking and make a list

Physical Health

What things that when you put into your body can make you more prone to experience a fight or flight response (anxiety, stress, overthinking)? Foods, stimulants, drinks, etc.

Physical Environment

What things in your physical environment can make you more prone to experience a fight or flight response (anxiety, stress, overthinking)?

Digital Environment

What things on your phone, computer, or TV can make you more prone to experience a fight or flight response (anxiety, stress, overthinking)?

Digital Consumption

What media/content when you consume can make you more prone to experience a fight or flight response (anxiety, stress, overthinking)?

Step 2: Reorganize & Rank Your Thinking Triggers

After filling out each category, go back in the worksheet to organize and identify the top 3 triggers that affect you the most within each category. Put a number from 1-3 to beside each of those triggers starting with #1 being the one that affects you most.

Check this box once you've gone back and ranked the top 3 triggers for each category

Step 3: Identify and implement ideas

Within each category, list the top trigger that affects you the most. Then use your intuition to come up with a way for you to remove or greatly minimize the trigger without it causing more stress, write it down, and a date for when you will implement it.

Physical Health

Top Trigger   Date:

Action Item

Physical Environment

Top Trigger   Date:

Action Item

Digital Environment

Top Trigger   Date:

Action Item

Digital Consumption

Top Trigger   Date:

Action Item

Step 4: Journal your insights and discoveries

Write down any insights you had while going through this specific exercise. What did you become aware of while going through it? What surprised you? What patterns did you notice? What does it cost you to continue to have these triggers in your life? What would happen if you removed them? What intentions would you like to set? Tune into your body and feel these answers to integrate it into your being.

CREATE A NON-THINKING ENVIRONMENT

Use your intuition and ask yourself this question:

"What would be the most impactful things I can do to help myself get into and maintain a peaceful, non-thinking state throughout my whole day?"

Write down any and all ideas that come to mind and don't filter anything. Allow your intuition to speak to you and tune into what feels most aligned with you. After writing down all of your ideas, go back and choose 1-3 ideas that feel most intuitively aligned with you to implement. Begin integrating those ideas into your life right now.

Additional Ideas For Creating A Non-thinking Environment

Write down all of the things that help you get into a relaxed, peaceful, non-thinking state. After completing each category, circle the most impactful item you can begin doing now.

Physical Health

Using your intuition, what comes to mind for things that you put in your body help you to feel healthy, sustainably energized, and peaceful?

Physical Environment

Using your intuition, what comes to mind for things in physical environment that help you get into a relaxed and peaceful non-thinking state?

Digital Environment

Using your intuition, what comes to mind for things on your phone or computer help you feel most aligned with your highest self?

Digital Consumption

What media/content you consume helps you to feel aligned with your highest self?

APPLYING NON-THINKING TO WORK

Use your intuition and ask yourself this question:

"What would be the most impactful things I can do to help myself get into and maintain a peaceful, non-thinking state throughout my whole day?"

Write down any and all ideas that come to mind and don't filter anything. Allow your intuition to speak to you and tune into what feels most aligned with you. After writing down all of your ideas, go back and choose 1-3 ideas that feel most intuitively aligned with you to implement. Begin integrating those ideas into your life right now.

DAILY JOURNALS

DAILY INTENTIONS

Without a conscious intention to follow our intuition, we default to following our conditioning. This daily journal is designed to help you break free from thinking and conditioning through bringing your intuition into your awareness. Becoming aware of your intuition and following it is the most important thing you can do for your own peace, happiness & fulfillment each day.

What is my intuition telling me today?

When I ignore external influences and advice from anyone else, what does my intuition tell me to move towards? What is my intuition it telling me to try? What feels most expansive, unknown, and aligned right now?

When I encounter fear & uncertainty (the unknown) today, how will I handle it?

Write a mantra to help you remember to trust & follow your intuition today.

DAILY REFLECTIONS

These reflection questions are designed to help you become aware of the inputs and causes of your level of peace, love, and joy in life. Positive emotions are our natural state when we let go of our thinking. Notice what happens when you focus your attention on the inputs instead of the outputs and how the outputs take care of themselves when you do so.

Input/Cause Questions

Rated on a scale of 1-10 with 1 being the lowest and 10 being the highest.

Rate 1-10

How much thinking did I do today?

How much did I follow my intuition today?

How much did I express my full, authentic self today?

How well did I manage my energy today?

How much did I follow what felt expansive, unknown, and aligned today?

Did I focus most of my attention on fully and unapologetically expressing myself or on external outcomes?

Circle One

Expressing myself   External Outcomes

Output/Effect Questions

Rated on a scale of 1-10 with 1 being the lowest and 10 being the highest.

Level of peace

Level of joy

Level of stress/anxiety

Level of alignment

How often was I in the present moment today?

How much was I in flow today?

Notice the correlation between the inputs and outputs. What comes up for you after answering these questions? What is your intuition telling you right now?

DAILY INTENTIONS

Without a conscious intention to follow our intuition, we default to following our conditioning. This daily journal is designed to help you break free from thinking and conditioning through bringing your intuition into your awareness. Becoming aware of your intuition and following it is the most important thing you can do for your own peace, happiness & fulfillment each day.

What is my intuition telling me today?

When I ignore external influences and advice from anyone else, what does my intuition tell me to move towards? What is my intuition it telling me to try? What feels most expansive, unknown, and aligned right now?

When I encounter fear & uncertainty (the unknown) today, how will I handle it?

Write a mantra to help you remember to trust & follow your intuition today.

DAILY REFLECTIONS

These reflection questions are designed to help you become aware of the inputs and causes of your level of peace, love, and joy in life. Positive emotions are our natural state when we let go of our thinking. Notice what happens when you focus your attention on the inputs instead of the outputs and how the outputs take care of themselves when you do so.

Input/Cause Questions
Rated on a scale of 1-10 with 1 being the lowest and 10 being the highest.

Rate 1-10

How much thinking did I do today?

How much did I follow my intuition today?

How much did I express my full, authentic self today?

How well did I manage my energy today?

How much did I follow what felt expansive, unknown, and aligned today?

Did I focus most of my attention on fully and unapologetically expressing myself or on external outcomes?

Circle One

Expressing myself   External Outcomes

Output/Effect Questions
Rated on a scale of 1-10 with 1 being the lowest and 10 being the highest.

Level of peace

Level of joy

Level of stress/anxiety

Level of alignment

How often was I in the present moment today?

How much was I in flow today?

Notice the correlation between the inputs and outputs. What comes up for you after answering these questions? What is your intuition telling you right now?

INTUITION JOURNAL – MORNING

DAILY INTENTIONS

Without a conscious intention to follow our intuition, we default to following our conditioning. This daily journal is designed to help you break free from thinking and conditioning through bringing your intuition into your awareness. Becoming aware of your intuition and following it is the most important thing you can do for your own peace, happiness & fulfillment each day.

What is my intuition telling me today?

When I ignore external influences and advice from anyone else, what does my intuition tell me to move towards? What is my intuition it telling me to try? What feels most expansive, unknown, and aligned right now?

When I encounter fear & uncertainty (the unknown) today, how will I handle it?

Write a mantra to help you remember to trust & follow your intuition today.

INTUITION JOURNAL - EVENING

DAILY REFLECTIONS

These reflection questions are designed to help you become aware of the inputs and causes of your level of peace, love, and joy in life. Positive emotions are our natural state when we let go of our thinking. Notice what happens when you focus your attention on the inputs instead of the outputs and how the outputs take care of themselves when you do so.

Input/Cause Questions

Rated on a scale of 1-10 with 1 being the lowest and 10 being the highest.

Rate 1-10

How much thinking did I do today?

How much did I follow my intuition today?

How much did I express my full, authentic self today?

How well did I manage my energy today?

How much did I follow what felt expansive, unknown, and aligned today?

Did I focus most of my attention on fully and unapologetically expressing myself or on external outcomes?

Circle One

Expressing myself   External Outcomes

Output/Effect Questions

Rated on a scale of 1-10 with 1 being the lowest and 10 being the highest.

Level of peace

Level of joy

Level of stress/anxiety

Level of alignment

How often was I in the present moment today?

How much was I in flow today?

Notice the correlation between the inputs and outputs. What comes up for you after answering these questions? What is your intuition telling you right now?

INTUITION JOURNAL – MORNING

DAILY INTENTIONS

Without a conscious intention to follow our intuition, we default to following our conditioning. This daily journal is designed to help you break free from thinking and conditioning through bringing your intuition into your awareness. Becoming aware of your intuition and following it is the most important thing you can do for your own peace, happiness & fulfillment each day.

What is my intuition telling me today?
When I ignore external influences and advice from anyone else, what does my intuition tell me to move towards? What is my intuition it telling me to try? What feels most expansive, unknown, and aligned right now?

When I encounter fear & uncertainty (the unknown) today, how will I handle it?

Write a mantra to help you remember to trust & follow your intuition today.

INTUITION JOURNAL - EVENING

DAILY REFLECTIONS

These reflection questions are designed to help you become aware of the inputs and causes of your level of peace, love, and joy in life. Positive emotions are our natural state when we let go of our thinking. Notice what happens when you focus your attention on the inputs instead of the outputs and how the outputs take care of themselves when you do so.

Input/Cause Questions   Rate 1-10

Rated on a scale of 1-10 with 1 being the lowest and 10 being the highest.

How much thinking did I do today?

How much did I follow my intuition today?

How much did I express my full, authentic self today?

How well did I manage my energy today?

How much did I follow what felt expansive, unknown, and aligned today?

Did I focus most of my attention on fully and unapologetically expressing myself or on external outcomes?

Circle One

Expressing myself   External Outcomes

Output/Effect Questions

Rated on a scale of 1-10 with 1 being the lowest and 10 being the highest.

Level of peace

Level of joy

Level of stress/anxiety

Level of alignment

How often was I in the present moment today?

How much was I in flow today?

Notice the correlation between the inputs and outputs. What comes up for you after answering these questions? What is your intuition telling you right now?

INTUITION JOURNAL – MORNING

DAILY INTENTIONS

Without a conscious intention to follow our intuition, we default to following our conditioning. This daily journal is designed to help you break free from thinking and conditioning through bringing your intuition into your awareness. Becoming aware of your intuition and following it is the most important thing you can do for your own peace, happiness & fulfillment each day.

What is my intuition telling me today?

When I ignore external influences and advice from anyone else, what does my intuition tell me to move towards? What is my intuition it telling me to try? What feels most expansive, unknown, and aligned right now?

When I encounter fear & uncertainty (the unknown) today, how will I handle it?

Write a mantra to help you remember to trust & follow your intuition today.

INTUITION JOURNAL – EVENING

DAILY REFLECTIONS

These reflection questions are designed to help you become aware of the inputs and causes of your level of peace, love, and joy in life. Positive emotions are our natural state when we let go of our thinking. Notice what happens when you focus your attention on the inputs instead of the outputs and how the outputs take care of themselves when you do so.

Input/Cause Questions

Rated on a scale of 1-10 with 1 being the lowest and 10 being the highest.

Rate 1-10

How much thinking did I do today?

How much did I follow my intuition today?

How much did I express my full, authentic self today?

How well did I manage my energy today?

How much did I follow what felt expansive, unknown, and aligned today?

Did I focus most of my attention on fully and unapologetically expressing myself or on external outcomes?

Circle One

Expressing myself   External Outcomes

Output/Effect Questions

Rated on a scale of 1-10 with 1 being the lowest and 10 being the highest.

Level of peace

Level of joy

Level of stress/anxiety

Level of alignment

How often was I in the present moment today?

How much was I in flow today?

Notice the correlation between the inputs and outputs. What comes up for you after answering these questions? What is your intuition telling you right now?

DATE:

INTUITION JOURNAL - MORNING

DAILY INTENTIONS

Without a conscious intention to follow our intuition, we default to following our conditioning. This daily journal is designed to help you break free from thinking and conditioning through bringing your intuition into your awareness. Becoming aware of your intuition and following it is the most important thing you can do for your own peace, happiness & fulfillment each day.

What is my intuition telling me today?

When I ignore external influences and advice from anyone else, what does my intuition tell me to move towards? What is my intuition it telling me to try? What feels most expansive, unknown, and aligned right now?

When I encounter fear & uncertainty (the unknown) today, how will I handle it?

Write a mantra to help you remember to trust & follow your intuition today.

DAILY REFLECTIONS

These reflection questions are designed to help you become aware of the inputs and causes of your level of peace, love, and joy in life. Positive emotions are our natural state when we let go of our thinking. Notice what happens when you focus your attention on the inputs instead of the outputs and how the outputs take care of themselves when you do so.

Input/Cause Questions
Rated on a scale of 1-10 with 1 being the lowest and 10 being the highest.

Rate 1-10

How much thinking did I do today?

How much did I follow my intuition today?

How much did I express my full, authentic self today?

How well did I manage my energy today?

How much did I follow what felt expansive, unknown, and aligned today?

Did I focus most of my attention on fully and unapologetically expressing myself or on external outcomes?

Circle One

Expressing myself   External Outcomes

Output/Effect Questions
Rated on a scale of 1-10 with 1 being the lowest and 10 being the highest.

Level of peace

Level of joy

Level of stress/anxiety

Level of alignment

How often was I in the present moment today?

How much was I in flow today?

Notice the correlation between the inputs and outputs. What comes up for you after answering these questions? What is your intuition telling you right now?

DATE:

INTUITION JOURNAL – MORNING

DAILY INTENTIONS

Without a conscious intention to follow our intuition, we default to following our conditioning. This daily journal is designed to help you break free from thinking and conditioning through bringing your intuition into your awareness. Becoming aware of your intuition and following it is the most important thing you can do for your own peace, happiness & fulfillment each day.

What is my intuition telling me today?
When I ignore external influences and advice from anyone else, what does my intuition tell me to move towards? What is my intuition it telling me to try? What feels most expansive, unknown, and aligned right now?

When I encounter fear & uncertainty (the unknown) today, how will I handle it?

Write a mantra to help you remember to trust & follow your intuition today.

INTUITION JOURNAL - EVENING

DAILY REFLECTIONS

These reflection questions are designed to help you become aware of the inputs and causes of your level of peace, love, and joy in life. Positive emotions are our natural state when we let go of our thinking. Notice what happens when you focus your attention on the inputs instead of the outputs and how the outputs take care of themselves when you do so.

Input/Cause Questions
Rated on a scale of 1-10 with 1 being the lowest and 10 being the highest.

Rate 1-10

How much thinking did I do today?

How much did I follow my intuition today?

How much did I express my full, authentic self today?

How well did I manage my energy today?

How much did I follow what felt expansive, unknown, and aligned today?

Did I focus most of my attention on fully and unapologetically expressing myself or on external outcomes?

Circle One

Expressing myself   External Outcomes

Output/Effect Questions
Rated on a scale of 1-10 with 1 being the lowest and 10 being the highest.

Level of peace

Level of joy

Level of stress/anxiety

Level of alignment

How often was I in the present moment today?

How much was I in flow today?

Notice the correlation between the inputs and outputs. What comes up for you after answering these questions? What is your intuition telling you right now?

INTUITION JOURNAL – MORNING

DAILY INTENTIONS

Without a conscious intention to follow our intuition, we default to following our conditioning. This daily journal is designed to help you break free from thinking and conditioning through bringing your intuition into your awareness. Becoming aware of your intuition and following it is the most important thing you can do for your own peace, happiness & fulfillment each day.

What is my intuition telling me today?

When I ignore external influences and advice from anyone else, what does my intuition tell me to move towards? What is my intuition it telling me to try? What feels most expansive, unknown, and aligned right now?

When I encounter fear & uncertainty (the unknown) today, how will I handle it?

Write a mantra to help you remember to trust & follow your intuition today.

DAILY REFLECTIONS

These reflection questions are designed to help you become aware of the inputs and causes of your level of peace, love, and joy in life. Positive emotions are our natural state when we let go of our thinking. Notice what happens when you focus your attention on the inputs instead of the outputs and how the outputs take care of themselves when you do so.

Input/Cause Questions   Rate 1-10
Rated on a scale of 1-10 with 1 being the lowest and 10 being the highest.

How much thinking did I do today?

How much did I follow my intuition today?

How much did I express my full, authentic self today?

How well did I manage my energy today?

How much did I follow what felt expansive, unknown, and aligned today?

Did I focus most of my attention on fully and unapologetically expressing myself or on external outcomes?

Circle One

Expressing myself   External Outcomes

Output/Effect Questions
Rated on a scale of 1-10 with 1 being the lowest and 10 being the highest.

Level of peace

Level of joy

Level of stress/anxiety

Level of alignment

How often was I in the present moment today?

How much was I in flow today?

Notice the correlation between the inputs and outputs. What comes up for you after answering these questions? What is your intuition telling you right now?

DAILY INTENTIONS

Without a conscious intention to follow our intuition, we default to following our conditioning. This daily journal is designed to help you break free from thinking and conditioning through bringing your intuition into your awareness. Becoming aware of your intuition and following it is the most important thing you can do for your own peace, happiness & fulfillment each day.

What is my intuition telling me today?
When I ignore external influences and advice from anyone else, what does my intuition tell me to move towards? What is my intuition it telling me to try? What feels most expansive, unknown, and aligned right now?

When I encounter fear & uncertainty (the unknown) today, how will I handle it?

Write a mantra to help you remember to trust & follow your intuition today.

DATE:

DAILY REFLECTIONS

These reflection questions are designed to help you become aware of the inputs and causes of your level of peace, love, and joy in life. Positive emotions are our natural state when we let go of our thinking. Notice what happens when you focus your attention on the inputs instead of the outputs and how the outputs take care of themselves when you do so.

Input/Cause Questions
Rated on a scale of 1-10 with 1 being the lowest and 10 being the highest.

Rate 1-10

How much thinking did I do today?

How much did I follow my intuition today?

How much did I express my full, authentic self today?

How well did I manage my energy today?

How much did I follow what felt expansive and unknown today?

Did I focus most of my attention on fully and unapologetically expressing myself or on external outcomes?

Circle One

Expressing myself   External Outcomes

Output/Effect Questions
Rated on a scale of 1-10 with 1 being the lowest and 10 being the highest.

Level of peace

Level of joy

Level of stress/anxiety

Level of alignment

How often was I in the present moment today?

How much was I in flow today?

Notice the correlation between the inputs and outputs. What comes up for you after answering these questions? What is your intuition telling you right now?

DAILY INTENTIONS

Without a conscious intention to follow our intuition, we default to following our conditioning. This daily journal is designed to help you break free from thinking and conditioning through bringing your intuition into your awareness. Becoming aware of your intuition and following it is the most important thing you can do for your own peace, happiness & fulfillment each day.

What is my intuition telling me today?
When I ignore external influences and advice from anyone else, what does my intuition tell me to move towards? What is my intuition it telling me to try? What feels most expansive, unknown, and aligned right now?

When I encounter fear & uncertainty (the unknown) today, how will I handle it?

Write a mantra to help you remember to trust & follow your intuition today.

INTUITION JOURNAL – EVENING

DAILY REFLECTIONS

These reflection questions are designed to help you become aware of the inputs and causes of your level of peace, love, and joy in life. Positive emotions are our natural state when we let go of our thinking. Notice what happens when you focus your attention on the inputs instead of the outputs and how the outputs take care of themselves when you do so.

Input/Cause Questions

Rated on a scale of 1-10 with 1 being the lowest and 10 being the highest.

Rate 1-10

How much thinking did I do today?

How much did I follow my intuition today?

How much did I express my full, authentic self today?

How well did I manage my energy today?

How much did I follow what felt expansive, unknown, and aligned today?

Did I focus most of my attention on fully and unapologetically expressing myself or on external outcomes?

Circle One

Expressing myself   External Outcomes

Output/Effect Questions

Rated on a scale of 1-10 with 1 being the lowest and 10 being the highest.

Level of peace

Level of joy

Level of stress/anxiety

Level of alignment

How often was I in the present moment today?

How much was I in flow today?

Notice the correlation between the inputs and outputs. What comes up for you after answering these questions? What is your intuition telling you right now?

INTUITION JOURNAL – MORNING

DAILY INTENTIONS

Without a conscious intention to follow our intuition, we default to following our conditioning. This daily journal is designed to help you break free from thinking and conditioning through bringing your intuition into your awareness. Becoming aware of your intuition and following it is the most important thing you can do for your own peace, happiness & fulfillment each day.

What is my intuition telling me today?
When I ignore external influences and advice from anyone else, what does my intuition tell me to move towards? What is my intuition it telling me to try? What feels most expansive, unknown, and aligned right now?

When I encounter fear & uncertainty (the unknown) today, how will I handle it?

Write a mantra to help you remember to trust & follow your intuition today.

INTUITION JOURNAL - EVENING

DAILY REFLECTIONS

These reflection questions are designed to help you become aware of the inputs and causes of your level of peace, love, and joy in life. Positive emotions are our natural state when we let go of our thinking. Notice what happens when you focus your attention on the inputs instead of the outputs and how the outputs take care of themselves when you do so.

Input/Cause Questions

Rated on a scale of 1-10 with 1 being the lowest and 10 being the highest.

Rate 1-10

How much thinking did I do today?

How much did I follow my intuition today?

How much did I express my full, authentic self today?

How well did I manage my energy today?

How much did I follow what felt expansive, unknown, and aligned today?

Did I focus most of my attention on fully and unapologetically expressing myself or on external outcomes?

Circle One

Expressing myself   External Outcomes

Output/Effect Questions

Rated on a scale of 1-10 with 1 being the lowest and 10 being the highest.

Level of peace

Level of joy

Level of stress/anxiety

Level of alignment

How often was I in the present moment today?

How much was I in flow today?

Notice the correlation between the inputs and outputs. What comes up for you after answering these questions? What is your intuition telling you right now?

DAILY INTENTIONS

Without a conscious intention to follow our intuition, we default to following our conditioning. This daily journal is designed to help you break free from thinking and conditioning through bringing your intuition into your awareness. Becoming aware of your intuition and following it is the most important thing you can do for your own peace, happiness & fulfillment each day.

What is my intuition telling me today?

When I ignore external influences and advice from anyone else, what does my intuition tell me to move towards? What is my intuition it telling me to try? What feels most expansive, unknown, and aligned right now?

When I encounter fear & uncertainty (the unknown) today, how will I handle it?

Write a mantra to help you remember to trust & follow your intuition today.

INTUITION JOURNAL - EVENING

DAILY REFLECTIONS

These reflection questions are designed to help you become aware of the inputs and causes of your level of peace, love, and joy in life. Positive emotions are our natural state when we let go of our thinking. Notice what happens when you focus your attention on the inputs instead of the outputs and how the outputs take care of themselves when you do so.

Input/Cause Questions
Rated on a scale of 1-10 with 1 being the lowest and 10 being the highest.

Rate 1-10

How much thinking did I do today?

How much did I follow my intuition today?

How much did I express my full, authentic self today?

How well did I manage my energy today?

How much did I follow what felt expansive, unknown, and aligned today?

Did I focus most of my attention on fully and unapologetically expressing myself or on external outcomes?

Circle One

Expressing myself   External Outcomes

Output/Effect Questions
Rated on a scale of 1-10 with 1 being the lowest and 10 being the highest.

Level of peace

Level of joy

Level of stress/anxiety

Level of alignment

How often was I in the present moment today?

How much was I in flow today?

Notice the correlation between the inputs and outputs. What comes up for you after answering these questions? What is your intuition telling you right now?

DATE:

INTUITION JOURNAL - MORNING

DAILY INTENTIONS

Without a conscious intention to follow our intuition, we default to following our conditioning. This daily journal is designed to help you break free from thinking and conditioning through bringing your intuition into your awareness. Becoming aware of your intuition and following it is the most important thing you can do for your own peace, happiness & fulfillment each day.

What is my intuition telling me today?
When I ignore external influences and advice from anyone else, what does my intuition tell me to move towards? What is my intuition it telling me to try? What feels most expansive, unknown, and aligned right now?

When I encounter fear & uncertainty (the unknown) today, how will I handle it?

Write a mantra to help you remember to trust & follow your intuition today.

DAILY REFLECTIONS

These reflection questions are designed to help you become aware of the inputs and causes of your level of peace, love, and joy in life. Positive emotions are our natural state when we let go of our thinking. Notice what happens when you focus your attention on the inputs instead of the outputs and how the outputs take care of themselves when you do so.

Input/Cause Questions
Rated on a scale of 1-10 with 1 being the lowest and 10 being the highest.

Rate 1-10

How much thinking did I do today?

How much did I follow my intuition today?

How much did I express my full, authentic self today?

How well did I manage my energy today?

How much did I follow what felt expansive, unknown, and aligned today?

Did I focus most of my attention on fully and unapologetically expressing myself or on external outcomes?

Circle One

Expressing myself   External Outcomes

Output/Effect Questions
Rated on a scale of 1-10 with 1 being the lowest and 10 being the highest.

Level of peace

Level of joy

Level of stress/anxiety

Level of alignment

How often was I in the present moment today?

How much was I in flow today?

Notice the correlation between the inputs and outputs. What comes up for you after answering these questions? What is your intuition telling you right now?

DAILY INTENTIONS

Without a conscious intention to follow our intuition, we default to following our conditioning. This daily journal is designed to help you break free from thinking and conditioning through bringing your intuition into your awareness. Becoming aware of your intuition and following it is the most important thing you can do for your own peace, happiness & fulfillment each day.

What is my intuition telling me today?

When I ignore external influences and advice from anyone else, what does my intuition tell me to move towards? What is my intuition it telling me to try? What feels most expansive, unknown, and aligned right now?

When I encounter fear & uncertainty (the unknown) today, how will I handle it?

Write a mantra to help you remember to trust & follow your intuition today.

DAILY REFLECTIONS

These reflection questions are designed to help you become aware of the inputs and causes of your level of peace, love, and joy in life. Positive emotions are our natural state when we let go of our thinking. Notice what happens when you focus your attention on the inputs instead of the outputs and how the outputs take care of themselves when you do so.

Input/Cause Questions

Rated on a scale of 1-10 with 1 being the lowest and 10 being the highest.

Rate 1-10

How much thinking did I do today?

How much did I follow my intuition today?

How much did I express my full, authentic self today?

How well did I manage my energy today?

How much did I follow what felt expansive, unknown, and aligned today?

Did I focus most of my attention on fully and unapologetically expressing myself or on external outcomes?

Circle One

Expressing myself   External Outcomes

Output/Effect Questions

Rated on a scale of 1-10 with 1 being the lowest and 10 being the highest.

Level of peace

Level of joy

Level of stress/anxiety

Level of alignment

How often was I in the present moment today?

How much was I in flow today?

Notice the correlation between the inputs and outputs. What comes up for you after answering these questions? What is your intuition telling you right now?

DAILY INTENTIONS

Without a conscious intention to follow our intuition, we default to following our conditioning. This daily journal is designed to help you break free from thinking and conditioning through bringing your intuition into your awareness. Becoming aware of your intuition and following it is the most important thing you can do for your own peace, happiness & fulfillment each day.

What is my intuition telling me today?

When I ignore external influences and advice from anyone else, what does my intuition tell me to move towards? What is my intuition it telling me to try? What feels most expansive, unknown, and aligned right now?

When I encounter fear & uncertainty (the unknown) today, how will I handle it?

Write a mantra to help you remember to trust & follow your intuition today.

INTUITION JOURNAL - EVENING

DAILY REFLECTIONS

These reflection questions are designed to help you become aware of the inputs and causes of your level of peace, love, and joy in life. Positive emotions are our natural state when we let go of our thinking. Notice what happens when you focus your attention on the inputs instead of the outputs and how the outputs take care of themselves when you do so.

Input/Cause Questions
Rated on a scale of 1-10 with 1 being the lowest and 10 being the highest.

Rate 1-10

How much thinking did I do today?

How much did I follow my intuition today?

How much did I express my full, authentic self today?

How well did I manage my energy today?

How much did I follow what felt expansive, unknown, and aligned today?

Did I focus most of my attention on fully and unapologetically expressing myself or on external outcomes?

Circle One

Expressing myself   External Outcomes

Output/Effect Questions
Rated on a scale of 1-10 with 1 being the lowest and 10 being the highest.

Level of peace

Level of joy

Level of stress/anxiety

Level of alignment

How often was I in the present moment today?

How much was I in flow today?

Notice the correlation between the inputs and outputs. What comes up for you after answering these questions? What is your intuition telling you right now?

DAILY INTENTIONS

Without a conscious intention to follow our intuition, we default to following our conditioning. This daily journal is designed to help you break free from thinking and conditioning through bringing your intuition into your awareness. Becoming aware of your intuition and following it is the most important thing you can do for your own peace, happiness & fulfillment each day.

What is my intuition telling me today?

When I ignore external influences and advice from anyone else, what does my intuition tell me to move towards? What is my intuition it telling me to try? What feels most expansive, unknown, and aligned right now?

When I encounter fear & uncertainty (the unknown) today, how will I handle it?

Write a mantra to help you remember to trust & follow your intuition today.

INTUITION JOURNAL - EVENING

DAILY REFLECTIONS

These reflection questions are designed to help you become aware of the inputs and causes of your level of peace, love, and joy in life. Positive emotions are our natural state when we let go of our thinking. Notice what happens when you focus your attention on the inputs instead of the outputs and how the outputs take care of themselves when you do so.

Input/Cause Questions

Rated on a scale of 1-10 with 1 being the lowest and 10 being the highest.

Rate 1-10

How much thinking did I do today?

How much did I follow my intuition today?

How much did I express my full, authentic self today?

How well did I manage my energy today?

How much did I follow what felt expansive, unknown, and aligned today?

Did I focus most of my attention on fully and unapologetically expressing myself or on external outcomes?

Circle One

Expressing myself   External Outcomes

Output/Effect Questions

Rated on a scale of 1-10 with 1 being the lowest and 10 being the highest.

Level of peace

Level of joy

Level of stress/anxiety

Level of alignment

How often was I in the present moment today?

How much was I in flow today?

Notice the correlation between the inputs and outputs. What comes up for you after answering these questions? What is your intuition telling you right now?

DAILY INTENTIONS

Without a conscious intention to follow our intuition, we default to following our conditioning. This daily journal is designed to help you break free from thinking and conditioning through bringing your intuition into your awareness. Becoming aware of your intuition and following it is the most important thing you can do for your own peace, happiness & fulfillment each day.

What is my intuition telling me today?

When I ignore external influences and advice from anyone else, what does my intuition tell me to move towards? What is my intuition it telling me to try? What feels most expansive, unknown, and aligned right now?

When I encounter fear & uncertainty (the unknown) today, how will I handle it?

Write a mantra to help you remember to trust & follow your intuition today.

DATE:

DAILY REFLECTIONS

These reflection questions are designed to help you become aware of the inputs and causes of your level of peace, love, and joy in life. Positive emotions are our natural state when we let go of our thinking. Notice what happens when you focus your attention on the inputs instead of the outputs and how the outputs take care of themselves when you do so.

Input/Cause Questions
Rated on a scale of 1-10 with 1 being the lowest and 10 being the highest.

Rate 1-10

How much thinking did I do today?

How much did I follow my intuition today?

How much did I express my full, authentic self today?

How well did I manage my energy today?

How much did I follow what felt expansive, unknown, and aligned today?

Did I focus most of my attention on fully and unapologetically expressing myself or on external outcomes?

Circle One

Expressing myself   External Outcomes

Output/Effect Questions
Rated on a scale of 1-10 with 1 being the lowest and 10 being the highest.

Level of peace

Level of joy

Level of stress/anxiety

Level of alignment

How often was I in the present moment today?

How much was I in flow today?

Notice the correlation between the inputs and outputs. What comes up for you after answering these questions? What is your intuition telling you right now?

INTUITION JOURNAL - MORNING

DAILY INTENTIONS

Without a conscious intention to follow our intuition, we default to following our conditioning. This daily journal is designed to help you break free from thinking and conditioning through bringing your intuition into your awareness. Becoming aware of your intuition and following it is the most important thing you can do for your own peace, happiness & fulfillment each day.

What is my intuition telling me today?

When I ignore external influences and advice from anyone else, what does my intuition tell me to move towards? What is my intuition it telling me to try? What feels most expansive, unknown, and aligned right now?

When I encounter fear & uncertainty (the unknown) today, how will I handle it?

Write a mantra to help you remember to trust & follow your intuition today.

DATE:

INTUITION JOURNAL - EVENING

DAILY REFLECTIONS

These reflection questions are designed to help you become aware of the inputs and causes of your level of peace, love, and joy in life. Positive emotions are our natural state when we let go of our thinking. Notice what happens when you focus your attention on the inputs instead of the outputs and how the outputs take care of themselves when you do so.

Input/Cause Questions
Rated on a scale of 1-10 with 1 being the lowest and 10 being the highest.

Rate 1-10

How much thinking did I do today?

How much did I follow my intuition today?

How much did I express my full, authentic self today?

How well did I manage my energy today?

How much did I follow what felt expansive, unknown, and aligned today?

Did I focus most of my attention on fully and unapologetically expressing myself or on external outcomes?

Circle One

Expressing myself   External Outcomes

Output/Effect Questions
Rated on a scale of 1-10 with 1 being the lowest and 10 being the highest.

Level of peace

Level of joy

Level of stress/anxiety

Level of alignment

How often was I in the present moment today?

How much was I in flow today?

Notice the correlation between the inputs and outputs. What comes up for you after answering these questions? What is your intuition telling you right now?

165

DAILY INTENTIONS

Without a conscious intention to follow our intuition, we default to following our conditioning. This daily journal is designed to help you break free from thinking and conditioning through bringing your intuition into your awareness. Becoming aware of your intuition and following it is the most important thing you can do for your own peace, happiness & fulfillment each day.

What is my intuition telling me today?

When I ignore external influences and advice from anyone else, what does my intuition tell me to move towards? What is my intuition it telling me to try? What feels most expansive, unknown, and aligned right now?

When I encounter fear & uncertainty (the unknown) today, how will I handle it?

Write a mantra to help you remember to trust & follow your intuition today.

INTUITION JOURNAL - EVENING

DAILY REFLECTIONS

These reflection questions are designed to help you become aware of the inputs and causes of your level of peace, love, and joy in life. Positive emotions are our natural state when we let go of our thinking. Notice what happens when you focus your attention on the inputs instead of the outputs and how the outputs take care of themselves when you do so.

Input/Cause Questions
Rated on a scale of 1-10 with 1 being the lowest and 10 being the highest.

Rate 1-10

How much thinking did I do today?

How much did I follow my intuition today?

How much did I express my full, authentic self today?

How well did I manage my energy today?

How much did I follow what felt expansive, unknown, and aligned today?

Did I focus most of my attention on fully and unapologetically expressing myself or on external outcomes?

Circle One

Expressing myself   External Outcomes

Output/Effect Questions
Rated on a scale of 1-10 with 1 being the lowest and 10 being the highest.

Level of peace

Level of joy

Level of stress/anxiety

Level of alignment

How often was I in the present moment today?

How much was I in flow today?

Notice the correlation between the inputs and outputs. What comes up for you after answering these questions? What is your intuition telling you right now?

INTUITION JOURNAL - MORNING

DAILY INTENTIONS

Without a conscious intention to follow our intuition, we default to following our conditioning. This daily journal is designed to help you break free from thinking and conditioning through bringing your intuition into your awareness. Becoming aware of your intuition and following it is the most important thing you can do for your own peace, happiness & fulfillment each day.

What is my intuition telling me today?

When I ignore external influences and advice from anyone else, what does my intuition tell me to move towards? What is my intuition it telling me to try? What feels most expansive, unknown, and aligned right now?

When I encounter fear & uncertainty (the unknown) today, how will I handle it?

Write a mantra to help you remember to trust & follow your intuition today.

INTUITION JOURNAL – EVENING

DAILY REFLECTIONS

These reflection questions are designed to help you become aware of the inputs and causes of your level of peace, love, and joy in life. Positive emotions are our natural state when we let go of our thinking. Notice what happens when you focus your attention on the inputs instead of the outputs and how the outputs take care of themselves when you do so.

Input/Cause Questions

Rated on a scale of 1-10 with 1 being the lowest and 10 being the highest.

Rate 1-10

How much thinking did I do today?

How much did I follow my intuition today?

How much did I express my full, authentic self today?

How well did I manage my energy today?

How much did I follow what felt expansive, unknown, and aligned today?

Did I focus most of my attention on fully and unapologetically expressing myself or on external outcomes?

Circle One

Expressing myself   External Outcomes

Output/Effect Questions

Rated on a scale of 1-10 with 1 being the lowest and 10 being the highest.

Level of peace

Level of joy

Level of stress/anxiety

Level of alignment

How often was I in the present moment today?

How much was I in flow today?

Notice the correlation between the inputs and outputs. What comes up for you after answering these questions? What is your intuition telling you right now?

DATE:

INTUITION JOURNAL - MORNING

DAILY INTENTIONS

Without a conscious intention to follow our intuition, we default to following our conditioning. This daily journal is designed to help you break free from thinking and conditioning through bringing your intuition into your awareness. Becoming aware of your intuition and following it is the most important thing you can do for your own peace, happiness & fulfillment each day.

What is my intuition telling me today?
When I ignore external influences and advice from anyone else, what does my intuition tell me to move towards? What is my intuition it telling me to try? What feels most expansive, unknown, and aligned right now?

When I encounter fear & uncertainty (the unknown) today, how will I handle it?

Write a mantra to help you remember to trust & follow your intuition today.

INTUITION JOURNAL – EVENING

DAILY REFLECTIONS

These reflection questions are designed to help you become aware of the inputs and causes of your level of peace, love, and joy in life. Positive emotions are our natural state when we let go of our thinking. Notice what happens when you focus your attention on the inputs instead of the outputs and how the outputs take care of themselves when you do so.

Input/Cause Questions
Rated on a scale of 1-10 with 1 being the lowest and 10 being the highest.

Rate 1-10

How much thinking did I do today?

How much did I follow my intuition today?

How much did I express my full, authentic self today?

How well did I manage my energy today?

How much did I follow what felt expansive, unknown, and aligned today?

Did I focus most of my attention on fully and unapologetically expressing myself or on external outcomes?

Circle One

Expressing myself   External Outcomes

Output/Effect Questions
Rated on a scale of 1-10 with 1 being the lowest and 10 being the highest.

Level of peace

Level of joy

Level of stress/anxiety

Level of alignment

How often was I in the present moment today?

How much was I in flow today?

Notice the correlation between the inputs and outputs. What comes up for you after answering these questions? What is your intuition telling you right now?

DAILY INTENTIONS

Without a conscious intention to follow our intuition, we default to following our conditioning. This daily journal is designed to help you break free from thinking and conditioning through bringing your intuition into your awareness. Becoming aware of your intuition and following it is the most important thing you can do for your own peace, happiness & fulfillment each day.

What is my intuition telling me today?

When I ignore external influences and advice from anyone else, what does my intuition tell me to move towards? What is my intuition it telling me to try? What feels most expansive, unknown, and aligned right now?

When I encounter fear & uncertainty (the unknown) today, how will I handle it?

Write a mantra to help you remember to trust & follow your intuition today.

DAILY REFLECTIONS

These reflection questions are designed to help you become aware of the inputs and causes of your level of peace, love, and joy in life. Positive emotions are our natural state when we let go of our thinking. Notice what happens when you focus your attention on the inputs instead of the outputs and how the outputs take care of themselves when you do so.

Input/Cause Questions
Rated on a scale of 1-10 with 1 being the lowest and 10 being the highest.

Rate 1-10

How much thinking did I do today?

How much did I follow my intuition today?

How much did I express my full, authentic self today?

How well did I manage my energy today?

How much did I follow what felt expansive, unknown, and aligned today?

Did I focus most of my attention on fully and unapologetically expressing myself or on external outcomes?

Circle One

Expressing myself   External Outcomes

Output/Effect Questions
Rated on a scale of 1-10 with 1 being the lowest and 10 being the highest.

Level of peace

Level of joy

Level of stress/anxiety

Level of alignment

How often was I in the present moment today?

How much was I in flow today?

Notice the correlation between the inputs and outputs. What comes up for you after answering these questions? What is your intuition telling you right now?

DAILY INTENTIONS

Without a conscious intention to follow our intuition, we default to following our conditioning. This daily journal is designed to help you break free from thinking and conditioning through bringing your intuition into your awareness. Becoming aware of your intuition and following it is the most important thing you can do for your own peace, happiness & fulfillment each day.

What is my intuition telling me today?

When I ignore external influences and advice from anyone else, what does my intuition tell me to move towards? What is my intuition it telling me to try? What feels most expansive, unknown, and aligned right now?

When I encounter fear & uncertainty (the unknown) today, how will I handle it?

Write a mantra to help you remember to trust & follow your intuition today.

INTUITION JOURNAL - EVENING

DAILY REFLECTIONS

These reflection questions are designed to help you become aware of the inputs and causes of your level of peace, love, and joy in life. Positive emotions are our natural state when we let go of our thinking. Notice what happens when you focus your attention on the inputs instead of the outputs and how the outputs take care of themselves when you do so.

Input/Cause Questions
Rated on a scale of 1-10 with 1 being the lowest and 10 being the highest.

Rate 1-10

How much thinking did I do today?

How much did I follow my intuition today?

How much did I express my full, authentic self today?

How well did I manage my energy today?

How much did I follow what felt expansive, unknown, and aligned today?

Did I focus most of my attention on fully and unapologetically expressing myself or on external outcomes?

Circle One

Expressing myself   External Outcomes

Output/Effect Questions
Rated on a scale of 1-10 with 1 being the lowest and 10 being the highest.

Level of peace

Level of joy

Level of stress/anxiety

Level of alignment

How often was I in the present moment today?

How much was I in flow today?

Notice the correlation between the inputs and outputs. What comes up for you after answering these questions? What is your intuition telling you right now?

INTUITION JOURNAL – MORNING

DAILY INTENTIONS

Without a conscious intention to follow our intuition, we default to following our conditioning. This daily journal is designed to help you break free from thinking and conditioning through bringing your intuition into your awareness. Becoming aware of your intuition and following it is the most important thing you can do for your own peace, happiness & fulfillment each day.

What is my intuition telling me today?

When I ignore external influences and advice from anyone else, what does my intuition tell me to move towards? What is my intuition it telling me to try? What feels most expansive, unknown, and aligned right now?

When I encounter fear & uncertainty (the unknown) today, how will I handle it?

Write a mantra to help you remember to trust & follow your intuition today.

INTUITION JOURNAL - EVENING

DAILY REFLECTIONS

These reflection questions are designed to help you become aware of the inputs and causes of your level of peace, love, and joy in life. Positive emotions are our natural state when we let go of our thinking. Notice what happens when you focus your attention on the inputs instead of the outputs and how the outputs take care of themselves when you do so.

Input/Cause Questions
Rated on a scale of 1-10 with 1 being the lowest and 10 being the highest.

Rate 1-10

How much thinking did I do today?

How much did I follow my intuition today?

How much did I express my full, authentic self today?

How well did I manage my energy today?

How much did I follow what felt expansive, unknown, and aligned today?

Did I focus most of my attention on fully and unapologetically expressing myself or on external outcomes?

Circle One

Expressing myself   External Outcomes

Output/Effect Questions
Rated on a scale of 1-10 with 1 being the lowest and 10 being the highest.

Level of peace

Level of joy

Level of stress/anxiety

Level of alignment

How often was I in the present moment today?

How much was I in flow today?

Notice the correlation between the inputs and outputs. What comes up for you after answering these questions? What is your intuition telling you right now?

DAILY INTENTIONS

Without a conscious intention to follow our intuition, we default to following our conditioning. This daily journal is designed to help you break free from thinking and conditioning through bringing your intuition into your awareness. Becoming aware of your intuition and following it is the most important thing you can do for your own peace, happiness & fulfillment each day.

What is my intuition telling me today?

When I ignore external influences and advice from anyone else, what does my intuition tell me to move towards? What is my intuition it telling me to try? What feels most expansive, unknown, and aligned right now?

When I encounter fear & uncertainty (the unknown) today, how will I handle it?

Write a mantra to help you remember to trust & follow your intuition today.

INTUITION JOURNAL - EVENING

DAILY REFLECTIONS

These reflection questions are designed to help you become aware of the inputs and causes of your level of peace, love, and joy in life. Positive emotions are our natural state when we let go of our thinking. Notice what happens when you focus your attention on the inputs instead of the outputs and how the outputs take care of themselves when you do so.

Input/Cause Questions   Rate 1-10
Rated on a scale of 1-10 with 1 being the lowest and 10 being the highest.

How much thinking did I do today?

How much did I follow my intuition today?

How much did I express my full, authentic self today?

How well did I manage my energy today?

How much did I follow what felt expansive, unknown, and aligned today?

Did I focus most of my attention on fully and
unapologetically expressing myself or on external
outcomes?

Circle One

Expressing myself   External Outcomes

Output/Effect Questions
Rated on a scale of 1-10 with 1 being the lowest and 10 being the highest.

Level of peace

Level of joy

Level of stress/anxiety

Level of alignment

How often was I in the present
moment today?

How much was I in flow today?

Notice the correlation between the inputs and outputs. What comes up for you after answering these questions? What is your intuition telling you right now?

INTUITION JOURNAL - MORNING

DAILY INTENTIONS

Without a conscious intention to follow our intuition, we default to following our conditioning. This daily journal is designed to help you break free from thinking and conditioning through bringing your intuition into your awareness. Becoming aware of your intuition and following it is the most important thing you can do for your own peace, happiness & fulfillment each day.

What is my intuition telling me today?

When I ignore external influences and advice from anyone else, what does my intuition tell me to move towards? What is my intuition it telling me to try? What feels most expansive, unknown, and aligned right now?

When I encounter fear & uncertainty (the unknown) today, how will I handle it?

Write a mantra to help you remember to trust & follow your intuition today.

INTUITION JOURNAL - EVENING

DAILY REFLECTIONS

These reflection questions are designed to help you become aware of the inputs and causes of your level of peace, love, and joy in life. Positive emotions are our natural state when we let go of our thinking. Notice what happens when you focus your attention on the inputs instead of the outputs and how the outputs take care of themselves when you do so.

Input/Cause Questions
Rated on a scale of 1-10 with 1 being the lowest and 10 being the highest.

Rate 1-10

How much thinking did I do today?

How much did I follow my intuition today?

How much did I express my full, authentic self today?

How well did I manage my energy today?

How much did I follow what felt expansive, unknown, and aligned today?

Did I focus most of my attention on fully and unapologetically expressing myself or on external outcomes?

Circle One

Expressing myself   External Outcomes

Output/Effect Questions
Rated on a scale of 1-10 with 1 being the lowest and 10 being the highest.

Level of peace

Level of joy

Level of stress/anxiety

Level of alignment

How often was I in the present moment today?

How much was I in flow today?

Notice the correlation between the inputs and outputs. What comes up for you after answering these questions? What is your intuition telling you right now?

DATE:

DAILY INTENTIONS

Without a conscious intention to follow our intuition, we default to following our conditioning. This daily journal is designed to help you break free from thinking and conditioning through bringing your intuition into your awareness. Becoming aware of your intuition and following it is the most important thing you can do for your own peace, happiness & fulfillment each day.

What is my intuition telling me today?
When I ignore external influences and advice from anyone else, what does my intuition tell me to move towards? What is my intuition it telling me to try? What feels most expansive, unknown, and aligned right now?

When I encounter fear & uncertainty (the unknown) today, how will I handle it?

Write a mantra to help you remember to trust & follow your intuition today.

DAILY REFLECTIONS

These reflection questions are designed to help you become aware of the inputs and causes of your level of peace, love, and joy in life. Positive emotions are our natural state when we let go of our thinking. Notice what happens when you focus your attention on the inputs instead of the outputs and how the outputs take care of themselves when you do so.

Input/Cause Questions

Rated on a scale of 1-10 with 1 being the lowest and 10 being the highest.

Rate 1-10

How much thinking did I do today?

How much did I follow my intuition today?

How much did I express my full, authentic self today?

How well did I manage my energy today?

How much did I follow what felt expansive, unknown, and aligned today?

Did I focus most of my attention on fully and unapologetically expressing myself or on external outcomes?

Circle One

Expressing myself   External Outcomes

Output/Effect Questions

Rated on a scale of 1-10 with 1 being the lowest and 10 being the highest.

Level of peace

Level of joy

Level of stress/anxiety

Level of alignment

How often was I in the present moment today?

How much was I in flow today?

Notice the correlation between the inputs and outputs. What comes up for you after answering these questions? What is your intuition telling you right now?

DATE:

INTUITION JOURNAL – MORNING

DAILY INTENTIONS

Without a conscious intention to follow our intuition, we default to following our conditioning. This daily journal is designed to help you break free from thinking and conditioning through bringing your intuition into your awareness. Becoming aware of your intuition and following it is the most important thing you can do for your own peace, happiness & fulfillment each day.

What is my intuition telling me today?
When I ignore external influences and advice from anyone else, what does my intuition tell me to move towards? What is my intuition it telling me to try? What feels most expansive, unknown, and aligned right now?

When I encounter fear & uncertainty (the unknown) today, how will I handle it?

Write a mantra to help you remember to trust & follow your intuition today.

DATE:

INTUITION JOURNAL - EVENING

DAILY REFLECTIONS

These reflection questions are designed to help you become aware of the inputs and causes of your level of peace, love, and joy in life. Positive emotions are our natural state when we let go of our thinking. Notice what happens when you focus your attention on the inputs instead of the outputs and how the outputs take care of themselves when you do so.

Input/Cause Questions
Rated on a scale of 1-10 with 1 being the lowest and 10 being the highest.

Rate 1-10

How much thinking did I do today?

How much did I follow my intuition today?

How much did I express my full, authentic self today?

How well did I manage my energy today?

How much did I follow what felt expansive, unknown, and aligned today?

Did I focus most of my attention on fully and unapologetically expressing myself or on external outcomes?

Circle One

Expressing myself   External Outcomes

Output/Effect Questions
Rated on a scale of 1-10 with 1 being the lowest and 10 being the highest.

Level of peace

Level of joy

Level of stress/anxiety

Level of alignment

How often was I in the present moment today?

How much was I in flow today?

Notice the correlation between the inputs and outputs. What comes up for you after answering these questions? What is your intuition telling you right now?

185

DAILY INTENTIONS

Without a conscious intention to follow our intuition, we default to following our conditioning. This daily journal is designed to help you break free from thinking and conditioning through bringing your intuition into your awareness. Becoming aware of your intuition and following it is the most important thing you can do for your own peace, happiness & fulfillment each day.

What is my intuition telling me today?

When I ignore external influences and advice from anyone else, what does my intuition tell me to move towards? What is my intuition it telling me to try? What feels most expansive, unknown, and aligned right now?

When I encounter fear & uncertainty (the unknown) today, how will I handle it?

Write a mantra to help you remember to trust & follow your intuition today.

DAILY REFLECTIONS

These reflection questions are designed to help you become aware of the inputs and causes of your level of peace, love, and joy in life. Positive emotions are our natural state when we let go of our thinking. Notice what happens when you focus your attention on the inputs instead of the outputs and how the outputs take care of themselves when you do so.

Input/Cause Questions

Rated on a scale of 1-10 with 1 being the lowest and 10 being the highest.

Rate 1-10

How much thinking did I do today?

How much did I follow my intuition today?

How much did I express my full, authentic self today?

How well did I manage my energy today?

How much did I follow what felt expansive, unknown, and aligned today?

Did I focus most of my attention on fully and unapologetically expressing myself or on external outcomes?

Circle One

Expressing myself   External Outcomes

Output/Effect Questions

Rated on a scale of 1-10 with 1 being the lowest and 10 being the highest.

Level of peace

Level of joy

Level of stress/anxiety

Level of alignment

How often was I in the present moment today?

How much was I in flow today?

Notice the correlation between the inputs and outputs. What comes up for you after answering these questions? What is your intuition telling you right now?

DAILY INTENTIONS

Without a conscious intention to follow our intuition, we default to following our conditioning. This daily journal is designed to help you break free from thinking and conditioning through bringing your intuition into your awareness. Becoming aware of your intuition and following it is the most important thing you can do for your own peace, happiness & fulfillment each day.

What is my intuition telling me today?

When I ignore external influences and advice from anyone else, what does my intuition tell me to move towards? What is my intuition it telling me to try? What feels most expansive, unknown, and aligned right now?

When I encounter fear & uncertainty (the unknown) today, how will I handle it?

Write a mantra to help you remember to trust & follow your intuition today.

INTUITION JOURNAL - EVENING

DAILY REFLECTIONS

These reflection questions are designed to help you become aware of the inputs and causes of your level of peace, love, and joy in life. Positive emotions are our natural state when we let go of our thinking. Notice what happens when you focus your attention on the inputs instead of the outputs and how the outputs take care of themselves when you do so.

Input/Cause Questions   Rate 1-10
Rated on a scale of 1-10 with 1 being the lowest and 10 being the highest.

How much thinking did I do today?

How much did I follow my intuition today?

How much did I express my full, authentic self today?

How well did I manage my energy today?

How much did I follow what felt expansive, unknown, and aligned today?

Did I focus most of my attention on fully and   Circle One
unapologetically expressing myself or on external
outcomes?   Expressing myself   External Outcomes

Output/Effect Questions
Rated on a scale of 1-10 with 1 being the lowest and 10 being the highest.

Level of peace   Level of alignment

Level of joy   How often was I in the present
                                        moment today?

Level of stress/anxiety   How much was I in flow today?

Notice the correlation between the inputs and outputs. What comes up for you after answering these questions? What is your intuition telling you right now?

DAILY INTENTIONS

Without a conscious intention to follow our intuition, we default to following our conditioning. This daily journal is designed to help you break free from thinking and conditioning through bringing your intuition into your awareness. Becoming aware of your intuition and following it is the most important thing you can do for your own peace, happiness & fulfillment each day.

What is my intuition telling me today?

When I ignore external influences and advice from anyone else, what does my intuition tell me to move towards? What is my intuition it telling me to try? What feels most expansive, unknown, and aligned right now?

When I encounter fear & uncertainty (the unknown) today, how will I handle it?

Write a mantra to help you remember to trust & follow your intuition today.

INTUITION JOURNAL — EVENING

DAILY REFLECTIONS

These reflection questions are designed to help you become aware of the inputs and causes of your level of peace, love, and joy in life. Positive emotions are our natural state when we let go of our thinking. Notice what happens when you focus your attention on the inputs instead of the outputs and how the outputs take care of themselves when you do so.

Input/Cause Questions
Rated on a scale of 1-10 with 1 being the lowest and 10 being the highest.

Rate 1-10

How much thinking did I do today?

How much did I follow my intuition today?

How much did I express my full, authentic self today?

How well did I manage my energy today?

How much did I follow what felt expansive, unknown, and aligned today?

Did I focus most of my attention on fully and unapologetically expressing myself or on external outcomes?

Circle One

Expressing myself   External Outcomes

Output/Effect Questions
Rated on a scale of 1-10 with 1 being the lowest and 10 being the highest.

Level of peace

Level of joy

Level of stress/anxiety

Level of alignment

How often was I in the present moment today?

How much was I in flow today?

Notice the correlation between the inputs and outputs. What comes up for you after answering these questions? What is your intuition telling you right now?

INTUITION JOURNAL – MORNING

DAILY INTENTIONS

Without a conscious intention to follow our intuition, we default to following our conditioning. This daily journal is designed to help you break free from thinking and conditioning through bringing your intuition into your awareness. Becoming aware of your intuition and following it is the most important thing you can do for your own peace, happiness & fulfillment each day.

What is my intuition telling me today?

When I ignore external influences and advice from anyone else, what does my intuition tell me to move towards? What is my intuition it telling me to try? What feels most expansive, unknown, and aligned right now?

When I encounter fear & uncertainty (the unknown) today, how will I handle it?

Write a mantra to help you remember to trust & follow your intuition today.

INTUITION JOURNAL – EVENING

DAILY REFLECTIONS

These reflection questions are designed to help you become aware of the inputs and causes of your level of peace, love, and joy in life. Positive emotions are our natural state when we let go of our thinking. Notice what happens when you focus your attention on the inputs instead of the outputs and how the outputs take care of themselves when you do so.

Input/Cause Questions
Rated on a scale of 1-10 with 1 being the lowest and 10 being the highest.

Rate 1-10

How much thinking did I do today?

How much did I follow my intuition today?

How much did I express my full, authentic self today?

How well did I manage my energy today?

How much did I follow what felt expansive, unknown, and aligned today?

Did I focus most of my attention on fully and unapologetically expressing myself or on external outcomes?

Circle One

Expressing myself   External Outcomes

Output/Effect Questions
Rated on a scale of 1-10 with 1 being the lowest and 10 being the highest.

Level of peace

Level of joy

Level of stress/anxiety

Level of alignment

How often was I in the present moment today?

How much was I in flow today?

Notice the correlation between the inputs and outputs. What comes up for you after answering these questions? What is your intuition telling you right now?

DAILY INTENTIONS

Without a conscious intention to follow our intuition, we default to following our conditioning. This daily journal is designed to help you break free from thinking and conditioning through bringing your intuition into your awareness. Becoming aware of your intuition and following it is the most important thing you can do for your own peace, happiness & fulfillment each day.

What is my intuition telling me today?

When I ignore external influences and advice from anyone else, what does my intuition tell me to move towards? What is my intuition it telling me to try? What feels most expansive, unknown, and aligned right now?

When I encounter fear & uncertainty (the unknown) today, how will I handle it?

Write a mantra to help you remember to trust & follow your intuition today.

INTUITION JOURNAL - EVENING

DAILY REFLECTIONS

These reflection questions are designed to help you become aware of the inputs and causes of your level of peace, love, and joy in life. Positive emotions are our natural state when we let go of our thinking. Notice what happens when you focus your attention on the inputs instead of the outputs and how the outputs take care of themselves when you do so.

Input/Cause Questions
Rated on a scale of 1-10 with 1 being the lowest and 10 being the highest.

Rate 1-10

How much thinking did I do today?

How much did I follow my intuition today?

How much did I express my full, authentic self today?

How well did I manage my energy today?

How much did I follow what felt expansive, unknown, and aligned today?

Did I focus most of my attention on fully and unapologetically expressing myself or on external outcomes?

Circle One

Expressing myself   External Outcomes

Output/Effect Questions
Rated on a scale of 1-10 with 1 being the lowest and 10 being the highest.

Level of peace

Level of joy

Level of stress/anxiety

Level of alignment

How often was I in the present moment today?

How much was I in flow today?

Notice the correlation between the inputs and outputs. What comes up for you after answering these questions? What is your intuition telling you right now?

DAILY INTENTIONS

Without a conscious intention to follow our intuition, we default to following our conditioning. This daily journal is designed to help you break free from thinking and conditioning through bringing your intuition into your awareness. Becoming aware of your intuition and following it is the most important thing you can do for your own peace, happiness & fulfillment each day.

What is my intuition telling me today?

When I ignore external influences and advice from anyone else, what does my intuition tell me to move towards? What is my intuition it telling me to try? What feels most expansive, unknown, and aligned right now?

When I encounter fear & uncertainty (the unknown) today, how will I handle it?

Write a mantra to help you remember to trust & follow your intuition today.

DAILY REFLECTIONS

These reflection questions are designed to help you become aware of the inputs and causes of your level of peace, love, and joy in life. Positive emotions are our natural state when we let go of our thinking. Notice what happens when you focus your attention on the inputs instead of the outputs and how the outputs take care of themselves when you do so.

Input/Cause Questions

Rated on a scale of 1-10 with 1 being the lowest and 10 being the highest.

Rate 1-10

How much thinking did I do today?

How much did I follow my intuition today?

How much did I express my full, authentic self today?

How well did I manage my energy today?

How much did I follow what felt expansive, unknown, and aligned today?

Did I focus most of my attention on fully and unapologetically expressing myself or on external outcomes?

Circle One

Expressing myself   External Outcomes

Output/Effect Questions

Rated on a scale of 1-10 with 1 being the lowest and 10 being the highest.

Level of peace

Level of joy

Level of stress/anxiety

Level of alignment

How often was I in the present moment today?

How much was I in flow today?

Notice the correlation between the inputs and outputs. What comes up for you after answering these questions? What is your intuition telling you right now?

INTUITION JOURNAL – MORNING

DAILY INTENTIONS

Without a conscious intention to follow our intuition, we default to following our conditioning. This daily journal is designed to help you break free from thinking and conditioning through bringing your intuition into your awareness. Becoming aware of your intuition and following it is the most important thing you can do for your own peace, happiness & fulfillment each day.

What is my intuition telling me today?

When I ignore external influences and advice from anyone else, what does my intuition tell me to move towards? What is my intuition it telling me to try? What feels most expansive, unknown, and aligned right now?

When I encounter fear & uncertainty (the unknown) today, how will I handle it?

Write a mantra to help you remember to trust & follow your intuition today.

INTUITION JOURNAL – EVENING

DAILY REFLECTIONS

These reflection questions are designed to help you become aware of the inputs and causes of your level of peace, love, and joy in life. Positive emotions are our natural state when we let go of our thinking. Notice what happens when you focus your attention on the inputs instead of the outputs and how the outputs take care of themselves when you do so.

Input/Cause Questions
Rated on a scale of 1-10 with 1 being the lowest and 10 being the highest.

Rate 1-10

How much thinking did I do today?

How much did I follow my intuition today?

How much did I express my full, authentic self today?

How well did I manage my energy today?

How much did I follow what felt expansive and unknown today?

Did I focus most of my attention on fully and unapologetically expressing myself or on external outcomes?

Circle One

Expressing myself   External Outcomes

Output/Effect Questions
Rated on a scale of 1-10 with 1 being the lowest and 10 being the highest.

Level of peace

Level of joy

Level of stress/anxiety

Level of alignment

How often was I in the present moment today?

How much was I in flow today?

Notice the correlation between the inputs and outputs. What comes up for you after answering these questions? What is your intuition telling you right now?

DAILY INTENTIONS

Without a conscious intention to follow our intuition, we default to following our conditioning. This daily journal is designed to help you break free from thinking and conditioning through bringing your intuition into your awareness. Becoming aware of your intuition and following it is the most important thing you can do for your own peace, happiness & fulfillment each day.

What is my intuition telling me today?

When I ignore external influences and advice from anyone else, what does my intuition tell me to move towards? What is my intuition it telling me to try? What feels most expansive, unknown, and aligned right now?

When I encounter fear & uncertainty (the unknown) today, how will I handle it?

Write a mantra to help you remember to trust & follow your intuition today.

INTUITION JOURNAL - EVENING

DAILY REFLECTIONS

These reflection questions are designed to help you become aware of the inputs and causes of your level of peace, love, and joy in life. Positive emotions are our natural state when we let go of our thinking. Notice what happens when you focus your attention on the inputs instead of the outputs and how the outputs take care of themselves when you do so.

Input/Cause Questions
Rated on a scale of 1-10 with 1 being the lowest and 10 being the highest.

Rate 1-10

How much thinking did I do today?

How much did I follow my intuition today?

How much did I express my full, authentic self today?

How well did I manage my energy today?

How much did I follow what felt expansive, unknown, and aligned today?

Did I focus most of my attention on fully and unapologetically expressing myself or on external outcomes?

Circle One

Expressing myself   External Outcomes

Output/Effect Questions
Rated on a scale of 1-10 with 1 being the lowest and 10 being the highest.

Level of peace

Level of joy

Level of stress/anxiety

Level of alignment

How often was I in the present moment today?

How much was I in flow today?

Notice the correlation between the inputs and outputs. What comes up for you after answering these questions? What is your intuition telling you right now?

DAILY INTENTIONS

Without a conscious intention to follow our intuition, we default to following our conditioning. This daily journal is designed to help you break free from thinking and conditioning through bringing your intuition into your awareness. Becoming aware of your intuition and following it is the most important thing you can do for your own peace, happiness & fulfillment each day.

What is my intuition telling me today?

When I ignore external influences and advice from anyone else, what does my intuition tell me to move towards? What is my intuition it telling me to try? What feels most expansive, unknown, and aligned right now?

When I encounter fear & uncertainty (the unknown) today, how will I handle it?

Write a mantra to help you remember to trust & follow your intuition today.

INTUITION JOURNAL - EVENING

DAILY REFLECTIONS

These reflection questions are designed to help you become aware of the inputs and causes of your level of peace, love, and joy in life. Positive emotions are our natural state when we let go of our thinking. Notice what happens when you focus your attention on the inputs instead of the outputs and how the outputs take care of themselves when you do so.

Input/Cause Questions

Rated on a scale of 1-10 with 1 being the lowest and 10 being the highest.

Rate 1-10

How much thinking did I do today?

How much did I follow my intuition today?

How much did I express my full, authentic self today?

How well did I manage my energy today?

How much did I follow what felt expansive, unknown, and aligned today?

Did I focus most of my attention on fully and unapologetically expressing myself or on external outcomes?

Circle One

Expressing myself   External Outcomes

Output/Effect Questions

Rated on a scale of 1-10 with 1 being the lowest and 10 being the highest.

Level of peace

Level of joy

Level of stress/anxiety

Level of alignment

How often was I in the present moment today?

How much was I in flow today?

Notice the correlation between the inputs and outputs. What comes up for you after answering these questions? What is your intuition telling you right now?

DAILY INTENTIONS

Without a conscious intention to follow our intuition, we default to following our conditioning. This daily journal is designed to help you break free from thinking and conditioning through bringing your intuition into your awareness. Becoming aware of your intuition and following it is the most important thing you can do for your own peace, happiness & fulfillment each day.

What is my intuition telling me today?

When I ignore external influences and advice from anyone else, what does my intuition tell me to move towards? What is my intuition it telling me to try? What feels most expansive, unknown, and aligned right now?

When I encounter fear & uncertainty (the unknown) today, how will I handle it?

Write a mantra to help you remember to trust & follow your intuition today.

INTUITION JOURNAL – EVENING

DAILY REFLECTIONS

These reflection questions are designed to help you become aware of the inputs and causes of your level of peace, love, and joy in life. Positive emotions are our natural state when we let go of our thinking. Notice what happens when you focus your attention on the inputs instead of the outputs and how the outputs take care of themselves when you do so.

Input/Cause Questions
Rated on a scale of 1-10 with 1 being the lowest and 10 being the highest.

Rate 1-10

How much thinking did I do today?

How much did I follow my intuition today?

How much did I express my full, authentic self today?

How well did I manage my energy today?

How much did I follow what felt expansive, unknown, and aligned today?

Did I focus most of my attention on fully and unapologetically expressing myself or on external outcomes?

Circle One

Expressing myself   External Outcomes

Output/Effect Questions
Rated on a scale of 1-10 with 1 being the lowest and 10 being the highest.

Level of peace

Level of joy

Level of stress/anxiety

Level of alignment

How often was I in the present moment today?

How much was I in flow today?

Notice the correlation between the inputs and outputs. What comes up for you after answering these questions? What is your intuition telling you right now?

DAILY INTENTIONS

Without a conscious intention to follow our intuition, we default to following our conditioning. This daily journal is designed to help you break free from thinking and conditioning through bringing your intuition into your awareness. Becoming aware of your intuition and following it is the most important thing you can do for your own peace, happiness & fulfillment each day.

What is my intuition telling me today?

When I ignore external influences and advice from anyone else, what does my intuition tell me to move towards? What is my intuition it telling me to try? What feels most expansive, unknown, and aligned right now?

When I encounter fear & uncertainty (the unknown) today, how will I handle it?

Write a mantra to help you remember to trust & follow your intuition today.

INTUITION JOURNAL – EVENING

DAILY REFLECTIONS

These reflection questions are designed to help you become aware of the inputs and causes of your level of peace, love, and joy in life. Positive emotions are our natural state when we let go of our thinking. Notice what happens when you focus your attention on the inputs instead of the outputs and how the outputs take care of themselves when you do so.

Input/Cause Questions
Rated on a scale of 1-10 with 1 being the lowest and 10 being the highest.

Rate 1-10

How much thinking did I do today?

How much did I follow my intuition today?

How much did I express my full, authentic self today?

How well did I manage my energy today?

How much did I follow what felt expansive, unknown, and aligned today?

Did I focus most of my attention on fully and unapologetically expressing myself or on external outcomes?

Circle One

Expressing myself   External Outcomes

Output/Effect Questions
Rated on a scale of 1-10 with 1 being the lowest and 10 being the highest.

Level of peace

Level of joy

Level of stress/anxiety

Level of alignment

How often was I in the present moment today?

How much was I in flow today?

Notice the correlation between the inputs and outputs. What comes up for you after answering these questions? What is your intuition telling you right now?

DAILY INTENTIONS

Without a conscious intention to follow our intuition, we default to following our conditioning. This daily journal is designed to help you break free from thinking and conditioning through bringing your intuition into your awareness. Becoming aware of your intuition and following it is the most important thing you can do for your own peace, happiness & fulfillment each day.

What is my intuition telling me today?

When I ignore external influences and advice from anyone else, what does my intuition tell me to move towards? What is my intuition it telling me to try? What feels most expansive, unknown, and aligned right now?

When I encounter fear & uncertainty (the unknown) today, how will I handle it?

Write a mantra to help you remember to trust & follow your intuition today.

INTUITION JOURNAL – EVENING

DAILY REFLECTIONS

These reflection questions are designed to help you become aware of the inputs and causes of your level of peace, love, and joy in life. Positive emotions are our natural state when we let go of our thinking. Notice what happens when you focus your attention on the inputs instead of the outputs and how the outputs take care of themselves when you do so.

Input/Cause Questions
Rated on a scale of 1-10 with 1 being the lowest and 10 being the highest.

Rate 1-10

How much thinking did I do today?

How much did I follow my intuition today?

How much did I express my full, authentic self today?

How well did I manage my energy today?

How much did I follow what felt expansive, unknown, and aligned today?

Did I focus most of my attention on fully and unapologetically expressing myself or on external outcomes?

Circle One

Expressing myself   External Outcomes

Output/Effect Questions
Rated on a scale of 1-10 with 1 being the lowest and 10 being the highest.

Level of peace

Level of joy

Level of stress/anxiety

Level of alignment

How often was I in the present moment today?

How much was I in flow today?

Notice the correlation between the inputs and outputs. What comes up for you after answering these questions? What is your intuition telling you right now?

INTUITION JOURNAL – MORNING

DAILY INTENTIONS

Without a conscious intention to follow our intuition, we default to following our conditioning. This daily journal is designed to help you break free from thinking and conditioning through bringing your intuition into your awareness. Becoming aware of your intuition and following it is the most important thing you can do for your own peace, happiness & fulfillment each day.

What is my intuition telling me today?

When I ignore external influences and advice from anyone else, what does my intuition tell me to move towards? What is my intuition it telling me to try? What feels most expansive, unknown, and aligned right now?

When I encounter fear & uncertainty (the unknown) today, how will I handle it?

Write a mantra to help you remember to trust & follow your intuition today.

DATE:

INTUITION JOURNAL – EVENING

DAILY REFLECTIONS

These reflection questions are designed to help you become aware of the inputs and causes of your level of peace, love, and joy in life. Positive emotions are our natural state when we let go of our thinking. Notice what happens when you focus your attention on the inputs instead of the outputs and how the outputs take care of themselves when you do so.

Input/Cause Questions
Rated on a scale of 1-10 with 1 being the lowest and 10 being the highest.

Rate 1-10

How much thinking did I do today?

How much did I follow my intuition today?

How much did I express my full, authentic self today?

How well did I manage my energy today?

How much did I follow what felt expansive, unknown, and aligned today?

Did I focus most of my attention on fully and unapologetically expressing myself or on external outcomes?

Circle One

Expressing myself   External Outcomes

Output/Effect Questions
Rated on a scale of 1-10 with 1 being the lowest and 10 being the highest.

Level of peace

Level of joy

Level of stress/anxiety

Level of alignment

How often was I in the present moment today?

How much was I in flow today?

Notice the correlation between the inputs and outputs. What comes up for you after answering these questions? What is your intuition telling you right now?

DAILY INTENTIONS

Without a conscious intention to follow our intuition, we default to following our conditioning. This daily journal is designed to help you break free from thinking and conditioning through bringing your intuition into your awareness. Becoming aware of your intuition and following it is the most important thing you can do for your own peace, happiness & fulfillment each day.

What is my intuition telling me today?

When I ignore external influences and advice from anyone else, what does my intuition tell me to move towards? What is my intuition it telling me to try? What feels most expansive, unknown, and aligned right now?

When I encounter fear & uncertainty (the unknown) today, how will I handle it?

Write a mantra to help you remember to trust & follow your intuition today.

INTUITION JOURNAL - EVENING

DAILY REFLECTIONS

These reflection questions are designed to help you become aware of the inputs and causes of your level of peace, love, and joy in life. Positive emotions are our natural state when we let go of our thinking. Notice what happens when you focus your attention on the inputs instead of the outputs and how the outputs take care of themselves when you do so.

Input/Cause Questions   Rate 1-10

Rated on a scale of 1-10 with 1 being the lowest and 10 being the highest.

How much thinking did I do today?

How much did I follow my intuition today?

How much did I express my full, authentic self today?

How well did I manage my energy today?

How much did I follow what felt expansive, unknown, and aligned today?

Did I focus most of my attention on fully and unapologetically expressing myself or on external outcomes?

Circle One

Expressing myself   External Outcomes

Output/Effect Questions

Rated on a scale of 1-10 with 1 being the lowest and 10 being the highest.

Level of peace

Level of joy

Level of stress/anxiety

Level of alignment

How often was I in the present moment today?

How much was I in flow today?

Notice the correlation between the inputs and outputs. What comes up for you after answering these questions? What is your intuition telling you right now?

INTUITION JOURNAL – MORNING

DAILY INTENTIONS

Without a conscious intention to follow our intuition, we default to following our conditioning. This daily journal is designed to help you break free from thinking and conditioning through bringing your intuition into your awareness. Becoming aware of your intuition and following it is the most important thing you can do for your own peace, happiness & fulfillment each day.

What is my intuition telling me today?

When I ignore external influences and advice from anyone else, what does my intuition tell me to move towards? What is my intuition it telling me to try? What feels most expansive, unknown, and aligned right now?

When I encounter fear & uncertainty (the unknown) today, how will I handle it?

Write a mantra to help you remember to trust & follow your intuition today.

INTUITION JOURNAL - EVENING

DAILY REFLECTIONS

These reflection questions are designed to help you become aware of the inputs and causes of your level of peace, love, and joy in life. Positive emotions are our natural state when we let go of our thinking. Notice what happens when you focus your attention on the inputs instead of the outputs and how the outputs take care of themselves when you do so.

Input/Cause Questions
Rated on a scale of 1-10 with 1 being the lowest and 10 being the highest.

Rate 1-10

How much thinking did I do today?

How much did I follow my intuition today?

How much did I express my full, authentic self today?

How well did I manage my energy today?

How much did I follow what felt expansive, unknown, and aligned today?

Did I focus most of my attention on fully and unapologetically expressing myself or on external outcomes?

Circle One

Expressing myself   External Outcomes

Output/Effect Questions
Rated on a scale of 1-10 with 1 being the lowest and 10 being the highest.

Level of peace

Level of joy

Level of stress/anxiety

Level of alignment

How often was I in the present moment today?

How much was I in flow today?

Notice the correlation between the inputs and outputs. What comes up for you after answering these questions? What is your intuition telling you right now?

DAILY INTENTIONS

Without a conscious intention to follow our intuition, we default to following our conditioning. This daily journal is designed to help you break free from thinking and conditioning through bringing your intuition into your awareness. Becoming aware of your intuition and following it is the most important thing you can do for your own peace, happiness & fulfillment each day.

What is my intuition telling me today?

When I ignore external influences and advice from anyone else, what does my intuition tell me to move towards? What is my intuition it telling me to try? What feels most expansive, unknown, and aligned right now?

When I encounter fear & uncertainty (the unknown) today, how will I handle it?

Write a mantra to help you remember to trust & follow your intuition today.

INTUITION JOURNAL - EVENING

DAILY REFLECTIONS

These reflection questions are designed to help you become aware of the inputs and causes of your level of peace, love, and joy in life. Positive emotions are our natural state when we let go of our thinking. Notice what happens when you focus your attention on the inputs instead of the outputs and how the outputs take care of themselves when you do so.

Input/Cause Questions
Rated on a scale of 1-10 with 1 being the lowest and 10 being the highest.

Rate 1-10

How much thinking did I do today?

How much did I follow my intuition today?

How much did I express my full, authentic self today?

How well did I manage my energy today?

How much did I follow what felt expansive, unknown, and aligned today?

Did I focus most of my attention on fully and unapologetically expressing myself or on external outcomes?

Circle One

Expressing myself   External Outcomes

Output/Effect Questions
Rated on a scale of 1-10 with 1 being the lowest and 10 being the highest.

Level of peace

Level of joy

Level of stress/anxiety

Level of alignment

How often was I in the present moment today?

How much was I in flow today?

Notice the correlation between the inputs and outputs. What comes up for you after answering these questions? What is your intuition telling you right now?

DATE:

INTUITION JOURNAL - MORNING

DAILY INTENTIONS

Without a conscious intention to follow our intuition, we default to following our conditioning. This daily journal is designed to help you break free from thinking and conditioning through bringing your intuition into your awareness. Becoming aware of your intuition and following it is the most important thing you can do for your own peace, happiness & fulfillment each day.

What is my intuition telling me today?
When I ignore external influences and advice from anyone else, what does my intuition tell me to move towards? What is my intuition it telling me to try? What feels most expansive, unknown, and aligned right now?

When I encounter fear & uncertainty (the unknown) today, how will I handle it?

Write a mantra to help you remember to trust & follow your intuition today.

DAILY REFLECTIONS

These reflection questions are designed to help you become aware of the inputs and causes of your level of peace, love, and joy in life. Positive emotions are our natural state when we let go of our thinking. Notice what happens when you focus your attention on the inputs instead of the outputs and how the outputs take care of themselves when you do so.

Input/Cause Questions

Rated on a scale of 1-10 with 1 being the lowest and 10 being the highest.

Rate 1-10

How much thinking did I do today?

How much did I follow my intuition today?

How much did I express my full, authentic self today?

How well did I manage my energy today?

How much did I follow what felt expansive, unknown, and aligned today?

Did I focus most of my attention on fully and unapologetically expressing myself or on external outcomes?

Circle One

Expressing myself   External Outcomes

Output/Effect Questions

Rated on a scale of 1-10 with 1 being the lowest and 10 being the highest.

Level of peace

Level of joy

Level of stress/anxiety

Level of alignment

How often was I in the present moment today?

How much was I in flow today?

Notice the correlation between the inputs and outputs. What comes up for you after answering these questions? What is your intuition telling you right now?

DAILY INTENTIONS

Without a conscious intention to follow our intuition, we default to following our conditioning. This daily journal is designed to help you break free from thinking and conditioning through bringing your intuition into your awareness. Becoming aware of your intuition and following it is the most important thing you can do for your own peace, happiness & fulfillment each day.

What is my intuition telling me today?

When I ignore external influences and advice from anyone else, what does my intuition tell me to move towards? What is my intuition it telling me to try? What feels most expansive, unknown, and aligned right now?

When I encounter fear & uncertainty (the unknown) today, how will I handle it?

Write a mantra to help you remember to trust & follow your intuition today.

DATE:

DAILY REFLECTIONS

These reflection questions are designed to help you become aware of the inputs and causes of your level of peace, love, and joy in life. Positive emotions are our natural state when we let go of our thinking. Notice what happens when you focus your attention on the inputs instead of the outputs and how the outputs take care of themselves when you do so.

Input/Cause Questions
Rated on a scale of 1-10 with 1 being the lowest and 10 being the highest.

Rate 1-10

How much thinking did I do today?

How much did I follow my intuition today?

How much did I express my full, authentic self today?

How well did I manage my energy today?

How much did I follow what felt expansive, unknown, and aligned today?

Did I focus most of my attention on fully and unapologetically expressing myself or on external outcomes?

Circle One

Expressing myself   External Outcomes

Output/Effect Questions
Rated on a scale of 1-10 with 1 being the lowest and 10 being the highest.

Level of peace

Level of joy

Level of stress/anxiety

Level of alignment

How often was I in the present moment today?

How much was I in flow today?

Notice the correlation between the inputs and outputs. What comes up for you after answering these questions? What is your intuition telling you right now?

INTUITION JOURNAL – MORNING

DAILY INTENTIONS

Without a conscious intention to follow our intuition, we default to following our conditioning. This daily journal is designed to help you break free from thinking and conditioning through bringing your intuition into your awareness. Becoming aware of your intuition and following it is the most important thing you can do for your own peace, happiness & fulfillment each day.

What is my intuition telling me today?

When I ignore external influences and advice from anyone else, what does my intuition tell me to move towards? What is my intuition it telling me to try? What feels most expansive, unknown, and aligned right now?

When I encounter fear & uncertainty (the unknown) today, how will I handle it?

Write a mantra to help you remember to trust & follow your intuition today.

DATE:

INTUITION JOURNAL - EVENING

DAILY REFLECTIONS

These reflection questions are designed to help you become aware of the inputs and causes of your level of peace, love, and joy in life. Positive emotions are our natural state when we let go of our thinking. Notice what happens when you focus your attention on the inputs instead of the outputs and how the outputs take care of themselves when you do so.

Input/Cause Questions
Rated on a scale of 1-10 with 1 being the lowest and 10 being the highest.

Rate 1-10

How much thinking did I do today?

How much did I follow my intuition today?

How much did I express my full, authentic self today?

How well did I manage my energy today?

How much did I follow what felt expansive, unknown, and aligned today?

Did I focus most of my attention on fully and unapologetically expressing myself or on external outcomes?

Circle One

Expressing myself   External Outcomes

Output/Effect Questions
Rated on a scale of 1-10 with 1 being the lowest and 10 being the highest.

Level of peace

Level of joy

Level of stress/anxiety

Level of alignment

How often was I in the present moment today?

How much was I in flow today?

Notice the correlation between the inputs and outputs. What comes up for you after answering these questions? What is your intuition telling you right now?

DAILY INTENTIONS

Without a conscious intention to follow our intuition, we default to following our conditioning. This daily journal is designed to help you break free from thinking and conditioning through bringing your intuition into your awareness. Becoming aware of your intuition and following it is the most important thing you can do for your own peace, happiness & fulfillment each day.

What is my intuition telling me today?
When I ignore external influences and advice from anyone else, what does my intuition tell me to move towards? What is my intuition it telling me to try? What feels most expansive, unknown, and aligned right now?

When I encounter fear & uncertainty (the unknown) today, how will I handle it?

Write a mantra to help you remember to trust & follow your intuition today.

INTUITION JOURNAL – EVENING

DAILY REFLECTIONS

These reflection questions are designed to help you become aware of the inputs and causes of your level of peace, love, and joy in life. Positive emotions are our natural state when we let go of our thinking. Notice what happens when you focus your attention on the inputs instead of the outputs and how the outputs take care of themselves when you do so.

Input/Cause Questions

Rated on a scale of 1-10 with 1 being the lowest and 10 being the highest.

Rate 1-10

How much thinking did I do today?

How much did I follow my intuition today?

How much did I express my full, authentic self today?

How well did I manage my energy today?

How much did I follow what felt expansive, unknown, and aligned today?

Did I focus most of my attention on fully and unapologetically expressing myself or on external outcomes?

Circle One

Expressing myself   External Outcomes

Output/Effect Questions

Rated on a scale of 1-10 with 1 being the lowest and 10 being the highest.

Level of peace

Level of joy

Level of stress/anxiety

Level of alignment

How often was I in the present moment today?

How much was I in flow today?

Notice the correlation between the inputs and outputs. What comes up for you after answering these questions? What is your intuition telling you right now?

DAILY INTENTIONS

Without a conscious intention to follow our intuition, we default to following our conditioning. This daily journal is designed to help you break free from thinking and conditioning through bringing your intuition into your awareness. Becoming aware of your intuition and following it is the most important thing you can do for your own peace, happiness & fulfillment each day.

What is my intuition telling me today?

When I ignore external influences and advice from anyone else, what does my intuition tell me to move towards? What is my intuition it telling me to try? What feels most expansive, unknown, and aligned right now?

When I encounter fear & uncertainty (the unknown) today, how will I handle it?

Write a mantra to help you remember to trust & follow your intuition today.

INTUITION JOURNAL - EVENING

DAILY REFLECTIONS

These reflection questions are designed to help you become aware of the inputs and causes of your level of peace, love, and joy in life. Positive emotions are our natural state when we let go of our thinking. Notice what happens when you focus your attention on the inputs instead of the outputs and how the outputs take care of themselves when you do so.

Input/Cause Questions
Rated on a scale of 1-10 with 1 being the lowest and 10 being the highest.

Rate 1-10

How much thinking did I do today?

How much did I follow my intuition today?

How much did I express my full, authentic self today?

How well did I manage my energy today?

How much did I follow what felt expansive, unknown, and aligned today?

Did I focus most of my attention on fully and unapologetically expressing myself or on external outcomes?

Circle One

Expressing myself   External Outcomes

Output/Effect Questions
Rated on a scale of 1-10 with 1 being the lowest and 10 being the highest.

Level of peace

Level of joy

Level of stress/anxiety

Level of alignment

How often was I in the present moment today?

How much was I in flow today?

Notice the correlation between the inputs and outputs. What comes up for you after answering these questions? What is your intuition telling you right now?

DAILY INTENTIONS

Without a conscious intention to follow our intuition, we default to following our conditioning. This daily journal is designed to help you break free from thinking and conditioning through bringing your intuition into your awareness. Becoming aware of your intuition and following it is the most important thing you can do for your own peace, happiness & fulfillment each day.

What is my intuition telling me today?

When I ignore external influences and advice from anyone else, what does my intuition tell me to move towards? What is my intuition it telling me to try? What feels most expansive, unknown, and aligned right now?

When I encounter fear & uncertainty (the unknown) today, how will I handle it?

Write a mantra to help you remember to trust & follow your intuition today.

INTUITION JOURNAL – EVENING

DAILY REFLECTIONS

These reflection questions are designed to help you become aware of the inputs and causes of your level of peace, love, and joy in life. Positive emotions are our natural state when we let go of our thinking. Notice what happens when you focus your attention on the inputs instead of the outputs and how the outputs take care of themselves when you do so.

Input/Cause Questions   Rate 1-10
Rated on a scale of 1-10 with 1 being the lowest and 10 being the highest.

How much thinking did I do today?

How much did I follow my intuition today?

How much did I express my full, authentic self today?

How well did I manage my energy today?

How much did I follow what felt expansive, unknown, and aligned today?

Did I focus most of my attention on fully and unapologetically expressing myself or on external outcomes?

Circle One

Expressing myself   External Outcomes

Output/Effect Questions
Rated on a scale of 1-10 with 1 being the lowest and 10 being the highest.

Level of peace

Level of joy

Level of stress/anxiety

Level of alignment

How often was I in the present moment today?

How much was I in flow today?

Notice the correlation between the inputs and outputs. What comes up for you after answering these questions? What is your intuition telling you right now?

DAILY INTENTIONS

Without a conscious intention to follow our intuition, we default to following our conditioning. This daily journal is designed to help you break free from thinking and conditioning through bringing your intuition into your awareness. Becoming aware of your intuition and following it is the most important thing you can do for your own peace, happiness & fulfillment each day.

What is my intuition telling me today?

When I ignore external influences and advice from anyone else, what does my intuition tell me to move towards? What is my intuition it telling me to try? What feels most expansive, unknown, and aligned right now?

When I encounter fear & uncertainty (the unknown) today, how will I handle it?

Write a mantra to help you remember to trust & follow your intuition today.

INTUITION JOURNAL - EVENING

DAILY REFLECTIONS

These reflection questions are designed to help you become aware of the inputs and causes of your level of peace, love, and joy in life. Positive emotions are our natural state when we let go of our thinking. Notice what happens when you focus your attention on the inputs instead of the outputs and how the outputs take care of themselves when you do so.

Input/Cause Questions
Rated on a scale of 1-10 with 1 being the lowest and 10 being the highest.

Rate 1-10

How much thinking did I do today?

How much did I follow my intuition today?

How much did I express my full, authentic self today?

How well did I manage my energy today?

How much did I follow what felt expansive, unknown, and aligned today?

Did I focus most of my attention on fully and unapologetically expressing myself or on external outcomes?

Circle One

Expressing myself   External Outcomes

Output/Effect Questions
Rated on a scale of 1-10 with 1 being the lowest and 10 being the highest.

Level of peace

Level of joy

Level of stress/anxiety

Level of alignment

How often was I in the present moment today?

How much was I in flow today?

Notice the correlation between the inputs and outputs. What comes up for you after answering these questions? What is your intuition telling you right now?

INTUITION JOURNAL - MORNING

DAILY INTENTIONS

Without a conscious intention to follow our intuition, we default to following our conditioning. This daily journal is designed to help you break free from thinking and conditioning through bringing your intuition into your awareness. Becoming aware of your intuition and following it is the most important thing you can do for your own peace, happiness & fulfillment each day.

What is my intuition telling me today?

When I ignore external influences and advice from anyone else, what does my intuition tell me to move towards? What is my intuition it telling me to try? What feels most expansive, unknown, and aligned right now?

When I encounter fear & uncertainty (the unknown) today, how will I handle it?

Write a mantra to help you remember to trust & follow your intuition today.

DATE:

DAILY REFLECTIONS

These reflection questions are designed to help you become aware of the inputs and causes of your level of peace, love, and joy in life. Positive emotions are our natural state when we let go of our thinking. Notice what happens when you focus your attention on the inputs instead of the outputs and how the outputs take care of themselves when you do so.

Input/Cause Questions
Rated on a scale of 1-10 with 1 being the lowest and 10 being the highest.

Rate 1-10

How much thinking did I do today?

How much did I follow my intuition today?

How much did I express my full, authentic self today?

How well did I manage my energy today?

How much did I follow what felt expansive, unknown, and aligned today?

Did I focus most of my attention on fully and unapologetically expressing myself or on external outcomes?

Circle One

Expressing myself   External Outcomes

Output/Effect Questions
Rated on a scale of 1-10 with 1 being the lowest and 10 being the highest.

Level of peace

Level of joy

Level of stress/anxiety

Level of alignment

How often was I in the present moment today?

How much was I in flow today?

Notice the correlation between the inputs and outputs. What comes up for you after answering these questions? What is your intuition telling you right now?

DAILY INTENTIONS

Without a conscious intention to follow our intuition, we default to following our conditioning. This daily journal is designed to help you break free from thinking and conditioning through bringing your intuition into your awareness. Becoming aware of your intuition and following it is the most important thing you can do for your own peace, happiness & fulfillment each day.

What is my intuition telling me today?

When I ignore external influences and advice from anyone else, what does my intuition tell me to move towards? What is my intuition it telling me to try? What feels most expansive, unknown, and aligned right now?

When I encounter fear & uncertainty (the unknown) today, how will I handle it?

Write a mantra to help you remember to trust & follow your intuition today.

DATE:

DAILY REFLECTIONS

These reflection questions are designed to help you become aware of the inputs and causes of your level of peace, love, and joy in life. Positive emotions are our natural state when we let go of our thinking. Notice what happens when you focus your attention on the inputs instead of the outputs and how the outputs take care of themselves when you do so.

Input/Cause Questions
Rated on a scale of 1-10 with 1 being the lowest and 10 being the highest.

Rate 1-10

How much thinking did I do today?

How much did I follow my intuition today?

How much did I express my full, authentic self today?

How well did I manage my energy today?

How much did I follow what felt expansive, unknown, and aligned today?

Did I focus most of my attention on fully and unapologetically expressing myself or on external outcomes?

Circle One

Expressing myself   External Outcomes

Output/Effect Questions
Rated on a scale of 1-10 with 1 being the lowest and 10 being the highest.

Level of peace

Level of joy

Level of stress/anxiety

Level of alignment

How often was I in the present moment today?

How much was I in flow today?

Notice the correlation between the inputs and outputs. What comes up for you after answering these questions? What is your intuition telling you right now?

INTUITION JOURNAL - MORNING

DAILY INTENTIONS

Without a conscious intention to follow our intuition, we default to following our conditioning. This daily journal is designed to help you break free from thinking and conditioning through bringing your intuition into your awareness. Becoming aware of your intuition and following it is the most important thing you can do for your own peace, happiness & fulfillment each day.

What is my intuition telling me today?

When I ignore external influences and advice from anyone else, what does my intuition tell me to move towards? What is my intuition it telling me to try? What feels most expansive, unknown, and aligned right now?

When I encounter fear & uncertainty (the unknown) today, how will I handle it?

Write a mantra to help you remember to trust & follow your intuition today.

INTUITION JOURNAL – EVENING

DAILY REFLECTIONS

These reflection questions are designed to help you become aware of the inputs and causes of your level of peace, love, and joy in life. Positive emotions are our natural state when we let go of our thinking. Notice what happens when you focus your attention on the inputs instead of the outputs and how the outputs take care of themselves when you do so.

Input/Cause Questions
Rated on a scale of 1-10 with 1 being the lowest and 10 being the highest.

Rate 1-10

How much thinking did I do today?

How much did I follow my intuition today?

How much did I express my full, authentic self today?

How well did I manage my energy today?

How much did I follow what felt expansive, unknown, and aligned today?

Did I focus most of my attention on fully and unapologetically expressing myself or on external outcomes?

Circle One

Expressing myself   External Outcomes

Output/Effect Questions
Rated on a scale of 1-10 with 1 being the lowest and 10 being the highest.

Level of peace

Level of joy

Level of stress/anxiety

Level of alignment

How often was I in the present moment today?

How much was I in flow today?

Notice the correlation between the inputs and outputs. What comes up for you after answering these questions? What is your intuition telling you right now?

DAILY INTENTIONS

Without a conscious intention to follow our intuition, we default to following our conditioning. This daily journal is designed to help you break free from thinking and conditioning through bringing your intuition into your awareness. Becoming aware of your intuition and following it is the most important thing you can do for your own peace, happiness & fulfillment each day.

What is my intuition telling me today?

When I ignore external influences and advice from anyone else, what does my intuition tell me to move towards? What is my intuition it telling me to try? What feels most expansive, unknown, and aligned right now?

When I encounter fear & uncertainty (the unknown) today, how will I handle it?

Write a mantra to help you remember to trust & follow your intuition today.

INTUITION JOURNAL – EVENING

DAILY REFLECTIONS

These reflection questions are designed to help you become aware of the inputs and causes of your level of peace, love, and joy in life. Positive emotions are our natural state when we let go of our thinking. Notice what happens when you focus your attention on the inputs instead of the outputs and how the outputs take care of themselves when you do so.

Input/Cause Questions

Rated on a scale of 1-10 with 1 being the lowest and 10 being the highest.

Rate 1-10

How much thinking did I do today?

How much did I follow my intuition today?

How much did I express my full, authentic self today?

How well did I manage my energy today?

How much did I follow what felt expansive, unknown, and aligned today?

Did I focus most of my attention on fully and unapologetically expressing myself or on external outcomes?

Circle One

Expressing myself   External Outcomes

Output/Effect Questions

Rated on a scale of 1-10 with 1 being the lowest and 10 being the highest.

Level of peace

Level of joy

Level of stress/anxiety

Level of alignment

How often was I in the present moment today?

How much was I in flow today?

Notice the correlation between the inputs and outputs. What comes up for you after answering these questions? What is your intuition telling you right now?

INTUITION JOURNAL – MORNING

DAILY INTENTIONS

Without a conscious intention to follow our intuition, we default to following our conditioning. This daily journal is designed to help you break free from thinking and conditioning through bringing your intuition into your awareness. Becoming aware of your intuition and following it is the most important thing you can do for your own peace, happiness & fulfillment each day.

What is my intuition telling me today?

When I ignore external influences and advice from anyone else, what does my intuition tell me to move towards? What is my intuition it telling me to try? What feels most expansive, unknown, and aligned right now?

When I encounter fear & uncertainty (the unknown) today, how will I handle it?

Write a mantra to help you remember to trust & follow your intuition today.

DATE:

INTUITION JOURNAL – EVENING

DAILY REFLECTIONS

These reflection questions are designed to help you become aware of the inputs and causes of your level of peace, love, and joy in life. Positive emotions are our natural state when we let go of our thinking. Notice what happens when you focus your attention on the inputs instead of the outputs and how the outputs take care of themselves when you do so.

Input/Cause Questions
Rated on a scale of 1-10 with 1 being the lowest and 10 being the highest.

Rate 1-10

How much thinking did I do today?

How much did I follow my intuition today?

How much did I express my full, authentic self today?

How well did I manage my energy today?

How much did I follow what felt expansive, unknown, and aligned today?

Did I focus most of my attention on fully and unapologetically expressing myself or on external outcomes?

Circle One

Expressing myself   External Outcomes

Output/Effect Questions
Rated on a scale of 1-10 with 1 being the lowest and 10 being the highest.

Level of peace

Level of joy

Level of stress/anxiety

Level of alignment

How often was I in the present moment today?

How much was I in flow today?

Notice the correlation between the inputs and outputs. What comes up for you after answering these questions? What is your intuition telling you right now?

DAILY INTENTIONS

Without a conscious intention to follow our intuition, we default to following our conditioning. This daily journal is designed to help you break free from thinking and conditioning through bringing your intuition into your awareness. Becoming aware of your intuition and following it is the most important thing you can do for your own peace, happiness & fulfillment each day.

What is my intuition telling me today?

When I ignore external influences and advice from anyone else, what does my intuition tell me to move towards? What is my intuition it telling me to try? What feels most expansive, unknown, and aligned right now?

When I encounter fear & uncertainty (the unknown) today, how will I handle it?

Write a mantra to help you remember to trust & follow your intuition today.

INTUITION JOURNAL - EVENING

DAILY REFLECTIONS

These reflection questions are designed to help you become aware of the inputs and causes of your level of peace, love, and joy in life. Positive emotions are our natural state when we let go of our thinking. Notice what happens when you focus your attention on the inputs instead of the outputs and how the outputs take care of themselves when you do so.

Input/Cause Questions

Rated on a scale of 1-10 with 1 being the lowest and 10 being the highest.

Rate 1-10

How much thinking did I do today?

How much did I follow my intuition today?

How much did I express my full, authentic self today?

How well did I manage my energy today?

How much did I follow what felt expansive, unknown, and aligned today?

Did I focus most of my attention on fully and unapologetically expressing myself or on external outcomes?

Circle One

Expressing myself   External Outcomes

Output/Effect Questions

Rated on a scale of 1-10 with 1 being the lowest and 10 being the highest.

Level of peace

Level of joy

Level of stress/anxiety

Level of alignment

How often was I in the present moment today?

How much was I in flow today?

Notice the correlation between the inputs and outputs. What comes up for you after answering these questions? What is your intuition telling you right now?

DAILY INTENTIONS

Without a conscious intention to follow our intuition, we default to following our conditioning. This daily journal is designed to help you break free from thinking and conditioning through bringing your intuition into your awareness. Becoming aware of your intuition and following it is the most important thing you can do for your own peace, happiness & fulfillment each day.

What is my intuition telling me today?

When I ignore external influences and advice from anyone else, what does my intuition tell me to move towards? What is my intuition it telling me to try? What feels most expansive, unknown, and aligned right now?

When I encounter fear & uncertainty (the unknown) today, how will I handle it?

Write a mantra to help you remember to trust & follow your intuition today.

INTUITION JOURNAL - EVENING

DAILY REFLECTIONS

These reflection questions are designed to help you become aware of the inputs and causes of your level of peace, love, and joy in life. Positive emotions are our natural state when we let go of our thinking. Notice what happens when you focus your attention on the inputs instead of the outputs and how the outputs take care of themselves when you do so.

Input/Cause Questions
Rated on a scale of 1-10 with 1 being the lowest and 10 being the highest.

Rate 1-10

How much thinking did I do today?

How much did I follow my intuition today?

How much did I express my full, authentic self today?

How well did I manage my energy today?

How much did I follow what felt expansive, unknown, and aligned today?

Did I focus most of my attention on fully and unapologetically expressing myself or on external outcomes?

Circle One

Expressing myself   External Outcomes

Output/Effect Questions
Rated on a scale of 1-10 with 1 being the lowest and 10 being the highest.

Level of peace

Level of joy

Level of stress/anxiety

Level of alignment

How often was I in the present moment today?

How much was I in flow today?

Notice the correlation between the inputs and outputs. What comes up for you after answering these questions? What is your intuition telling you right now?

DAILY INTENTIONS

Without a conscious intention to follow our intuition, we default to following our conditioning. This daily journal is designed to help you break free from thinking and conditioning through bringing your intuition into your awareness. Becoming aware of your intuition and following it is the most important thing you can do for your own peace, happiness & fulfillment each day.

What is my intuition telling me today?

When I ignore external influences and advice from anyone else, what does my intuition tell me to move towards? What is my intuition it telling me to try? What feels most expansive, unknown, and aligned right now?

When I encounter fear & uncertainty (the unknown) today, how will I handle it?

Write a mantra to help you remember to trust & follow your intuition today.

INTUITION JOURNAL - EVENING

DAILY REFLECTIONS

These reflection questions are designed to help you become aware of the inputs and causes of your level of peace, love, and joy in life. Positive emotions are our natural state when we let go of our thinking. Notice what happens when you focus your attention on the inputs instead of the outputs and how the outputs take care of themselves when you do so.

Input/Cause Questions

Rated on a scale of 1-10 with 1 being the lowest and 10 being the highest.

Rate 1-10

How much thinking did I do today?

How much did I follow my intuition today?

How much did I express my full, authentic self today?

How well did I manage my energy today?

How much did I follow what felt expansive, unknown, and aligned today?

Did I focus most of my attention on fully and unapologetically expressing myself or on external outcomes?

Circle One

Expressing myself   External Outcomes

Output/Effect Questions

Rated on a scale of 1-10 with 1 being the lowest and 10 being the highest.

Level of peace

Level of joy

Level of stress/anxiety

Level of alignment

How often was I in the present moment today?

How much was I in flow today?

Notice the correlation between the inputs and outputs. What comes up for you after answering these questions? What is your intuition telling you right now?

DATE:

DAILY INTENTIONS

Without a conscious intention to follow our intuition, we default to following our conditioning. This daily journal is designed to help you break free from thinking and conditioning through bringing your intuition into your awareness. Becoming aware of your intuition and following it is the most important thing you can do for your own peace, happiness & fulfillment each day.

What is my intuition telling me today?

When I ignore external influences and advice from anyone else, what does my intuition tell me to move towards? What is my intuition it telling me to try? What feels most expansive, unknown, and aligned right now?

When I encounter fear & uncertainty (the unknown) today, how will I handle it?

Write a mantra to help you remember to trust & follow your intuition today.

INTUITION JOURNAL - EVENING

DAILY REFLECTIONS

These reflection questions are designed to help you become aware of the inputs and causes of your level of peace, love, and joy in life. Positive emotions are our natural state when we let go of our thinking. Notice what happens when you focus your attention on the inputs instead of the outputs and how the outputs take care of themselves when you do so.

Input/Cause Questions
Rated on a scale of 1-10 with 1 being the lowest and 10 being the highest.

Rate 1-10

How much thinking did I do today?

How much did I follow my intuition today?

How much did I express my full, authentic self today?

How well did I manage my energy today?

How much did I follow what felt expansive, unknown, and aligned today?

Did I focus most of my attention on fully and unapologetically expressing myself or on external outcomes?

Circle One

Expressing myself   External Outcomes

Output/Effect Questions
Rated on a scale of 1-10 with 1 being the lowest and 10 being the highest.

Level of peace

Level of joy

Level of stress/anxiety

Level of alignment

How often was I in the present moment today?

How much was I in flow today?

Notice the correlation between the inputs and outputs. What comes up for you after answering these questions? What is your intuition telling you right now?

ISBN: 979-8-9864065-2-7

First printing edition 2022 in United States

Made in United States
Orlando, FL
13 April 2025

60435314R00146